Also by Todd English and Sally Sampson

The Figs Table

The Olives Table

By Sally Sampson

The BakeSale Cookbook

The $50 Dinner Party

Recipes from the Night Kitchen

Simon & Schuster

NEW YORK   LONDON   TORONTO   SYDNEY   SINGAPORE

The Olives Dessert Table

SPECTACULAR RESTAURANT DESSERTS
YOU CAN MAKE AT HOME

Todd English, Paige Retus, and Sally Sampson

Photographs by Carl Tremblay

SIMON & SCHUSTER
Rockefeller Center
1230 Avenue of the Americas
New York, NY 10020

BOOK DESIGN BY DEBORAH KERNER

Manufactured in the United States of America
10 9 8 7 6 5 4 3 2 1
Library of Congress Cataloging-in-Publication Data
English, Todd.
    The Olives dessert table : spectacular restaurant desserts
you can make at home / Todd English, Paige Retus, and
Sally Sampson ; photography by Carl Tremblay.
        p.   cm.
Includes index.
    1. Desserts.   2. Olives Table (Restaurant).   I. Retus,
Paige.   II. Sampson, Sally, date.   III. Title.
TX773.E546 2000
641.8'6—dc21   00-044034

ISBN 978-1-5011-9071-1

ACKNOWLEDGMENTS

Thank you to Sydny Miner, Carla Glasser, and Beth Wareham, for all of the thoughtful consideration and extra care they brought to this project.

Thank you to right hand Maria Wharton, a careful and conscientious coworker who supports us endlessly. Thank you to a wonderful and very talented crew, past and present: Heather Macdonald, Melissa Ballantyne, Lauren Robinshaw, Barbara Caturano, and Julie Sebell. Assistants are not often in a position to take credit or catch a bit of the spotlight, but these people work diligently and with good spirit and it is very much appreciated.

Extra special thanks to Jesus Gutierez who constantly amazes us with his skill and attitude. As the single plater at Olives, Jesus is often under the gun to perform, and he always shines.

Thank you to Joe Brenner, who has steadfastly been a sounding board.

Thank you to the kitchen crew at Olives, who continually astound and challenge us.

Special thanks to the service staff at Olives. These folks make our jobs much more enjoyable. They also make them easier.

Thank you to the office staff, who always seem to have the answers.

Thank you also to all of the people we've worked with and for. We are a compilation of all of our experiences, all of the people we've been exposed to, and all of the places we've been to. This book is a reflection of all of you.

Special thanks to the following Boston-area stores for supplying the props for our photos: Bloomingdale's; Neiman Marcus; Shreve, Crump & Low; and Repertoire.

And last but not least, to the guests of Olives for their continued feedback and support. Without you, we would not be here.

To my wife, Olivia;

my uncle Placido,
who had a bakery in the Bronx
where I would go as a child
and stare at the blocks of butter
that were taller than me;

and my kids,
Oliver, Isabelle, and Simon,
who love to lick the bowls.

T.E.

For Ted

P.R.

For Mark, Lauren, and Ben

S.S.

Contents

Dreamy, Creamy Custards and Puddings and Tiramisu   67

BLACK-BOTTOMED CRÈME BRÛLÉE WITH CHEWY CHOCOLATE
CHIP COOKIES AND CHOCOLATE SAUCE *68*

GINGER BRÛLÉE WITH BURIED BLACKBERRIES, HOT AND SASSY
CAKES, AND BLACKBERRY CRUSH *73*

PUMPKIN GINGER CRÈME CARAMEL ON SPICED PUMPKIN CAKE
WITH PECAN SHORTS AND TOFFEED PECANS *78*

BUTTERSCOTCH PUDDING IN A CHOCOLATE CRUMB CRUST
WITH FUDGE-TOPPED TOFFEE COOKIES AND
CHOCOLATE LACE CIGARETTES *84*

APRICOT FLAN ON SHERRY-SPIKED MARQUISE WITH SHORTBREAD
CHECKERBOARDS AND DRIED-APRICOT SORBET *90*

BANANA-WHITE CHOCOLATE CRÈME CARAMEL
WITH BRÛLÉED BABY BANANAS ON A
TOFFEE-BOTTOMED COCOA CAKE *96*

ROASTED BANANA TIRAMISU *102*

Soufflés Are Not as Tough as You Think   111

VERY VANILLA BEAN SOUFFLÉ WITH VANILLA ANGLAISE,
VANILLA ICE CREAM, AND A TUILE TWIST *112*

DOUBLE CHOCOLATE SOUFFLÉ WITH DEEP, DARK CHOCOLATE
ICE CREAM, CHOCOLATE-CHOCOLATE CHIP COOKIES, AND
CHOCOLATE ANGLAISE *118*

PUMPKIN PIE SOUFFLÉ WITH HONEY LACE, CINNAMON ANGLAISE,
AND HAZELNUT-CRANBERRY RUGELACH *124*

FROZEN CITRUS "SOUFFLÉ" WITH LEMON CURD
AND CITRUS SHORTBREAD *132*

Seasonal Fruits and Tarts   137

FRESH FIG- AND RASPBERRY-STUDDED LEMON TART
   WITH COOLING BUTTERMILK "ICE CREAM"
   AND RASPBERRY CRUSH   *138*

BLUEBERRY-LIME TART WITH SWEET COCONUT CRUMBLE
   AND BLUEBERRY SORBET   *144*

NECTARINE-BLUEBERRY CRISP WITH OATMEAL CRUMBLE
   AND BUTTERMILK "ICE CREAM"   *150*

JOHNNYCAKE COBBLER WITH DARK BING CHERRIES
   AND MASCARPONE ICE CREAM   *154*

PLUM CROSTADA WITH MASCARPONE AND LEMON ICE CREAM   *157*

RASPBERRY BLUSH PEACH MELBA WITH ALMOND MADELEINES
   AND SWEET, TOASTY ALMONDS   *162*

WARM PLUM COMPOTE OVER WHITE CHOCOLATE ICE CREAM
   WITH PEPPERED-CANDIED WALNUTS AND WALNUT BISCOTTI   *167*

APRICOT AND GOAT CHEESE TART IN A PISTACHIO SHELL   *173*

CHOCOLATE-LACED CARAMELIZED HAZELNUT TART
   WITH CHOCOLATE SEMI-FREDDO AND HAZELNUT
   SANDWICH COOKIES   *176*

LIME AND MANGO TART WITH ZESTY LIME CURD
   AND BROILED MANGOES   *183*

BUTTER-BASTED APPLE TART WITH CURRANTS AND WALNUTS,
   CORNMEAL DOUGH, AND ZALETTI   *188*

LAYERED BANANA CREAM PIE WITH PECAN GOO ON SWEET
   BANANA CAKE WITH TOFFEED PECANS AND TUILES   *193*

MANGO TARTE TATIN WITH PASTRY CREAM
   AND CHOCOLATE PASTRY   *202*

Cakes 209

APPLE-TOPPED GINGERBREAD WITH HOT APPLESAUCE
AND CINNAMON ICE CREAM *210*

REAL GOOD, REAL BASIC POUND CAKE WITH SEASONAL FRUIT
COMPOTE AND BURNT ORANGE ICE CREAM *214*

CRANBERRY UPSIDE-DOWN CAKE WITH CARAMEL SEMI-FREDDO
AND PECAN SHORTS *220*

HOT AND SASSY GINGERBREAD WITH GINGER CRINKLES,
CIDER SAUCE, AND GINGER ICE CREAM *225*

MANY-LAYERED LEMON CAKE *233*

ESPRESSO TORTE *239*

Ice Cream and Sorbets 247

TURTLE SUNDAE: CARAMEL AND VANILLA BEAN ICE CREAMS
IN A PECAN SHORT SHELL WITH CHOCOLATE AND
CARAMEL SAUCES, SALTED PECAN BARK, CARAMEL
TURTLES, CHANTILLY CREAM, AND SALTED PECANS *248*

CRANBERRY-LIME SORBET WITH WALNUT RUGELACH *255*

LIME GRANITA WITH RASPBERRY CRUSH
AND CITRUS SHORTBREADS *259*

Cheese and Breads 263

BLUE CHEESE DANISH WITH PORT-POACHED PEARS *264*

CARAMELIZED WALNUT TART WITH PRUNES, ONIONS,
AND BLUE CHEESE *269*

GORGONZOLA BISCUITS WITH POACHED
PEAR REDUCTION *273*

INTRODUCTION

In the spring of 1997 Todd and I put the finishing touches on *The Figs Table*. I arrived at the restaurant one morning feigning interest in work, but in reality I was in hot pursuit of a great banana bread recipe. I asked Paige Retus, Olives' pastry chef, if she had one. She replied that hers was standard fare but, she said fortuitously, "You can see for yourself: I have some in the oven."

When the banana bread came out, she brought each of us a big fat steaming hunk. Todd and I were delirious with joy. We begged for more. We asked that she recite the recipe. The technique. In spite of the fact that we were swooning, Paige hadn't been wrong when she said "standard fare": There were no unusual ingredients, no bizarre techniques. The only difference was that Paige "whipped the bejesus out of the bananas." We decided at once that desserts would be the subject of our next book and Paige our collaborator.

When we tasted the banana bread, we realized that it was emblematic of what made the desserts at Olives so celebrated. It was the familiar made finer. Olives' desserts always begin with a simple recipe like banana bread. Brownies. Chocolate Cake. Butterscotch Pudding. Cookies. Bread Pudding. Shortbread. However elaborate they may seem, they are straightforward and accessible (though always better than mine and probably better than yours). They are fresher, they use higher quality ingredients, and the elements of each dessert are combined in ways that wouldn't occur to most people.

The philosophy for Olives' desserts is the same for Olives' entrées. "We like," says Todd, "to pull things out of the country and dress them up. We take very simple, often very common things and layer them together to compose a more complex dish." The outcome: desserts that always taste extravagant. Sinful. Comfortable. Unique yet familiar.

When Todd and Paige think about, talk about, and make dessert, they analyze, taste, discuss, and retaste each recipe to the point of obsession. They have access to ingredients, techniques, and equipment that the average person doesn't. Both are consumed with temperature, texture, and mouth feel. "Although I like," says Todd, "hot food to be hot and cold food to be cold, the truth is that you get maximum flavor when what you eat is close to your body temperature. It is then that food seems to have the best flavor."

But don't get me wrong: While Todd and Paige agree that their desserts must taste extraordinary, they don't always agree on what that constitutes.

Todd arrives with the ever-changing, wilder perspective of a cook, and Paige adds the scientific exactitude of a pastry chef. "Todd and I," says Paige, "work so well together because we have the same vision. He feeds me ideas and I use my practical experience to make them real. He's thinking of the finished product and I am thinking of how to get there." As a chef who works primarily with savory ingredients, Todd's inclination is to use ingredients that are not traditionally found in American desserts. Paige leans on what's familiar to her: classic sweet ingredients.

A world traveler, Todd is exposed to and inspired by a wide variety of foods. When he returns to Olives, he has big, new ideas and will try almost anything. Paige, on the other hand, has ingredients she considers "illegal." "I will," she admits, "use certain ingredients only under duress." Yet Todd respects that Paige has to play with some of his ideas before she can work the bugs out. And neither will do wacky for the sake of wacky. Most of Olives' desserts have roots in classic American and European desserts. They have to be familiar to taste good and they must strike home.

Olives' desserts stem from a respect for flavors rather than desserts that are visual masterpieces; you'll never have to dismantle a towering inferno or remove an inedible garnish. "A delicious but messed-up tiramisu," says Todd, "is more important than an architectural dessert that doesn't taste good. That's what people want."

And most important, the desserts have to equal the quality of the entrées. "Dessert," says Paige, "cannot be a letdown."

Now see for yourself: They never are.

HOW TO USE THIS BOOK

Please read before proceeding!

The desserts in this book are restaurant style, which means that they aim to dazzle. We know that you aren't going to make one of these recipes every night or even every week. We know that in this era of health consciousness, dessert is not a regular part of the family meal, so we feel that when it appears, it needs to be special.

At Olives, the many components of a dessert are made at different times and sometimes by different people. The same can be done in your own kitchen: You can make one component and freeze it, make another the day before, and yet another in the morning. You can buy the ice cream instead of churning it yourself.

It is not necessary to make any of these desserts in their entirety. All components that can stand alone are marked with this symbol: ✳ Make two Banana Breads. Eat one for breakfast and freeze the other for a future White Chocolate Banana Bread Pudding with Caramel Semi-Freddo and Boozy Caramel Sauce. Of course, you can skip the Semi-Freddo. Or skip the Semi-Freddo and the Caramel Sauce. Or serve the Caramel Sauce over store-bought vanilla ice cream. Just don't be intimidated. Make the Black-Bottomed Crème Brûlée with Chewy Chocolate Chip Cookies and Chocolate Sauce or just make the Chocolate Chip Cookies. Just don't be intimidated.

And if you do mess up, says Paige, you don't have to throw it out. If it's broken or imperfect, even if it's a cookie, break it up and put it in something else; add it to bars, to ice cream, or add it as a garnish.

We do, however, want you to buy the very best, very finest ingredients you can find. Where we have suggestions or a particular ingredient makes a difference to the finished dish, we have said so. If it is in your power to obtain them, please do. It will make a difference. You'll find a list of mail-order sources on page 277.

You may notice that we have repeated several recipes throughout the book. We hate cookbooks that endlessly refer you to other recipes, and since our lovely editor was willing, we figured we'd do anything to make this book more user-friendly. Now roll up your sleeves and have some fun.

The Olives Dessert Table

OLIVES' LAWS

These are the rules we go by (in no particular order) and if you follow them, you'll find that your desserts will be that much better.

1. Don't separate eggs with your hands. Go shell to shell.

2. Eggs are large and at room temperature.

3. Butter is unsalted.

4. Brown sugar is light brown unless specified, and tightly packed.

5. All nuts are toasted unless specified.

6. Milk always refers to whole milk. If you use skim or low fat, your desserts will suffer for it.

7. Use pure vanilla extract.

8. Use parchment paper liberally. Don't sweat the expense, you can reuse it.

9. Use the highest quality chocolate and cocoa you can find.

10. Scrub lemons, limes, and oranges before zesting.

11. Always have a perfectly clean bowl and whisk when whipping egg whites.

12. Fruit should be perfectly ripe; cooking won't ripen a rock-hard pear.

13. Ingredients should be at room temperature whenever possible.

14. Don't use ultrapasteurized cream. Pasteurized cream is harder to find but well worth the search.

ESSENTIAL INGREDIENTS

Pantry:

all-purpose flour
baking powder
baking soda
brown sugar, light
cake flour
chocolate
        bittersweet chocolate, Callebaut, El Rey, and Valrhona
        milk chocolate, El Rey
        semisweet chocolate, Callebaut
        unsweetened chocolate, Callebaut
        unsweetened cocoa powder, Valrhona
        white chocolate, El Rey

◆ SEMISWEET VERSUS BITTERSWEET CHOCOLATE SEMISWEET CHOCOLATE AND BITTERSWEET CHOCOLATE CAN, FOR THE MOST PART, BE USED INTERCHANGEABLY, ALTHOUGH WE GENERALLY PREFER BITTERSWEET, WHICH IS LESS SWEET. SUGAR CONTENT WILL VARY ACCORDING TO THE MANUFACTURER; THERE ARE NO HARD AND FAST RULES FOR PERCENTAGE OF SUGAR. ◆

coconut, shredded sweetened
confectioners' sugar
rolled oats, old-fashioned *not* quick cooking
pure granulated sugar
pure vanilla extract, such as Neilson Massey
table salt

Spices:

black pepper
ground cinnamon
ground ginger
vanilla beans

Refrigerator:

butter, unsalted
eggs, large
lemons
milk, whole
pecans
walnuts

ESSENTIAL EQUIPMENT

Equipment:

food processor
ice cream machine
KitchenAid mixer

Pots and Pans (nonreactive):

baking sheet without sides, 18 x 12 x 1 inches
2 round cake pans, 9 inches
8-inch-square cake pan
9 x 12-inch cake pan
loaf pans, 8 to 9 inches
mini muffin tins
tart pans, 9 inches

glass or ceramic mixing bowls, assorted sizes
stainless steel or plastic mixing bowls, assorted sizes
2-quart saucepan
3-quart saucepan

Other:

baker's spatula—also called an offset
candy thermometer
cooling racks

good resilient cutting board, wood or acrylic
ice cream scoops, nos. 100, 70, 40 (these mean scoops per
    quart); available at restaurant supply stores
kitchen timer
measuring cups, heavy-gauge stainless steel
measuring spoons, heavy-gauge stainless steel
oven thermometer
pot holders; dish towels
rolling pin
rubber spatulas, assorted sizes
sharp paring knife
vegetable peeler
whisks of many sizes
wooden spoons, assorted sizes

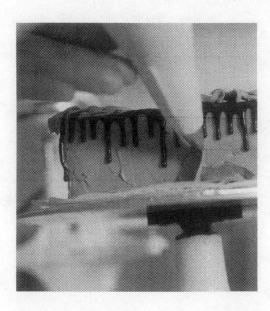

citrus juicer
citrus peeler
lemon zester

aluminum foil
beans, rice, or pie
    weights
parchment paper
plastic wrap

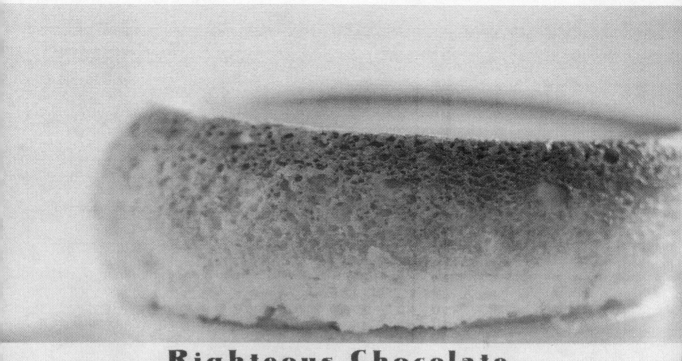

Righteous Chocolate

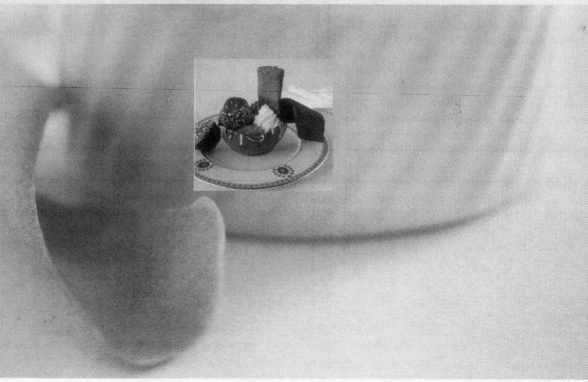

Falling Chocolate Cake
with Raspberry Sauce

ebbie Merriam, Olives' first baker, and Todd came up with this one together. It's never, ever been off the menu, and it never will be.

Raspberry Sauce

4 cups fresh or frozen raspberries
½ cup sugar
1 to 3 teaspoons fresh lemon juice

Place the raspberries and sugar in a small saucepan and bring to a boil, stirring, over high heat. Boil until the sugar dissolves. Add lemon juice to taste. Let cool.

Place half the sauce in a food processor fitted with a steel blade and puree. Combine with the remaining sauce, cover, and refrigerate until cold.

MAKES 3 CUPS

Chocolate Cake *

2 tablespoons unsalted butter, for preparing ramekins
2 tablespoons all-purpose flour, for preparing ramekins
12 ounces bittersweet chocolate, coarsely chopped
½ pound (2 sticks) unsalted butter
1 cup sugar
½ cup all-purpose flour
6 large eggs

4 cups Vanilla Bean Ice Cream (page 112) or other vanilla ice cream of
*   your choice, for serving*
2 tablespoons confectioners' sugar, for garnish
6 fresh mint sprigs, for garnish

Preheat the oven to 350 degrees. Generously butter and flour six 8-ounce ramekins.

Place the chocolate and butter in the top of a double boiler over simmering water. Stir until completely melted. Set aside to cool.

Place the sugar, flour, and eggs in a large bowl and beat until thick and fluffy, about 5 minutes. Gently beat in the cooled chocolate mixture.

Pour the batter into the prepared ramekins, filling them two-thirds to three-quarters of the way up the sides. Bake until they begin to puff up, about 15 minutes. Run a knife around the edge of each ramekin and turn the ramekin upside down on a plate to unmold.

TO FINISH AND ASSEMBLE:

1. Serve each warm cake surrounded by sauce, with a scoop of vanilla ice cream alongside.
2. Garnish with the confectioners' sugar and sprigs of fresh mint.

SERVES 6

Baked Chocolate Mousse on a Crunch Base with a Chocolate Tuile Fan and Chantilly Cream

The inspiration for this dessert was a baked chocolate mousse from The Baricelli Inn, a beautiful, quaint small inn in Cleveland, Ohio; it tasted fabulous but was fragile and hard to cut. When Paige was the pastry chef at One Market in San Francisco, she and chef Tony D'Ofrono stabilized the original recipe and added a textured chocolate crust. At Olives, Paige and Todd experimented with a higher quality chocolate and added the tuile fan. The result: a chocolate extravaganza of contrasting textures that will thrill the most jaded chocoholic. Use the best quality chocolate you can find; this is not the time to be frugal.

Chocolate Tuile Fan ✳

A tuile is a sweet, dry, crisp French cookie often made with crushed almonds. It is usually placed on a rolling pin, dowel, or broom handle just as it comes out of the oven to make it curve like a roof tile, hence its name. For this recipe we've fanned it to add height and drama to the presentation. Tuiles are great with coffee and store well in airtight container up to one week.

If you want a white cookie, simply substitute an equal amount of cornstarch for the cocoa powder.

¼ pound plus 2 tablespoons (1¼ sticks) unsalted butter, melted
1 cup confectioners' sugar
½ cup plus 2 tablespoons sugar
½ teaspoon vanilla extract
½ teaspoon almond extract
¼ teaspoon salt
5 large egg whites
⅔ cup plus 2 tablespoons all-purpose flour
⅓ cup unsweetened cocoa powder

Preheat the oven to 350 degrees. Line a baking sheet with parchment paper.

Place the butter and sugars in the bowl of a mixer fitted with a paddle and mix until smooth, creamy, and warm, but not hot, about 3 to 4 minutes. Add the vanilla, almond extract, and salt and mix until incorporated.

Add half the egg whites and mix until completely incorporated. Scrape down the bowl, add half the flour, and mix until completely incorporated. Scrape down the bowl, add the cocoa, and mix until completely incorporated. Scrape down the bowl and repeat with the remaining egg whites and flour. Cover and refrigerate until spreadable but not liquidy, about 30 minutes.

Place 1 teaspoonful of the mixture on the prepared baking sheet and, using the back of a spoon, form into a circle. Space 2 inches apart. Repeat until the baking sheet is full. Return the remaining mixture to the refrigerator.

Transfer the baking sheet to the oven and bake until the cookies are dry to the touch, about 8 minutes. Remove from the oven and immediately, one by one, pinch each tuile between 5 o'clock and 7 o'clock so that the bottom will ruffle and the top will fan out. Set aside to cool. Repeat with the remaining batter. Cool and place in an airtight container for up to 1 week.

Save 12 fans for the dessert garnish and break up the rest for the Crunch.

MAKES 24 TO 30 TUILES

Crunch

Crushed-up tuile and milk chocolate makes Olives' Crunch a grown-up candy crunch bar that is perfect for a snack, either cold or at room temperature.

Tuiles break easily. Broken cookies can be added to Espresso Buttercream (page 242) and used as a filling, or can be pressed into the sides of a finished cake to cover up imperfections.

Bittersweet chocolate can be substituted for the milk chocolate.

* HOT-WATER BATH POUR I INCH WATER IN A SMALL SAUCEPAN AND BRING TO A SIMMER OVER MEDIUM-LOW HEAT. DO NOT LET IT BOIL. PLACE A SMALL DRY MIXING BOWL INTO THE MOUTH OF THE PAN AND ADD THE INGREDIENTS YOU ARE TRYING TO MELT OR THICKEN. COOK AS DIRECTED IN THE INSTRUCTIONS. *

8 ounces milk chocolate, melted over a hot-water bath and cooled to room temperature

2 cups Chocolate Tuile Fan pieces (about 4 ounces); each piece should be about the size of a thumbnail

Line a baking sheet with parchment paper.

Place the chocolate in a mixing bowl and gently fold in the tuiles, taking care to coat all the surfaces.

Spread the mixture as thinly as possible onto the parchment paper and refrigerate until cooled. Cut out 12 circles using a 3- or 4-inch ring mold or for a single mousse cut out one circle using a 9- or 10-inch springform as a template (the Crunch can be covered and refrigerated for up to 1 week). Break up the remaining Crunch and use for a garnish.

MAKES 12 SMALL CIRCLES OR 1 LARGE CIRCLE PLUS GARNISH

Baked Chocolate Mousse ✳

This recipe calls for ring molds, which only the most serious bakers will have. Before you run out and buy them, try using water chestnut or tuna cans with both ends removed. Wash the cans extremely well, but if using tuna cans for a dessert is just too unpalatable to you, buy the molds at Williams-Sonoma or Sur La Table; they have a great selection.

The crunch base makes this easier to pick up, but you could certainly serve this as is. You could also use a cookie crust such as Toffee Dough (page 98) or Bitter Chocolate Shortbread (page 243): Roll out the cookie dough, cut out a circle, bake, and fit into the mold.

> 1 pound semisweet chocolate, such as Callebaut, Valrhona, or El Rey
> 6 tablespoons unsalted butter
> 1 cup heavy cream
> ¼ cup Kahlúa
> 6 large eggs, at room temperature
> ½ cup sugar
> ½ teaspoon salt

Preheat the oven to 325 degrees. Line twelve 3- to 4-inch ring molds or one 9- to 10-inch springform pan with parchment paper. Wrap the bottoms with plastic wrap and then again with aluminum foil as a precaution against water leaking in.

Place the chocolate and butter in a double boiler and cook over medium heat until both have melted. Set aside to cool.

Place the cream and Kahlúa in the bowl of a mixer fitted with a whip and whip until stiff peaks form. Cover and refrigerate.

Place the eggs, sugar, and salt in a large mixing bowl and whip on low speed for 2 minutes. Increase the speed to medium and whip for 2 minutes. Increase the speed to high and whip until the mixture climbs the side of the bowl and leaves tracks (will have the consistency of really soft whipped cream), about an additional 4 minutes. After it has grown as much as it can, it will begin to recede and lose volume. Stop beating immediately and gently fold the cooled chocolate mixture and the cream mixture into the egg mixture by hand.

Fit a circle of Crunch onto the bottom of each prepared mold (if it doesn't fit perfectly, don't worry, it will melt and reset). Divide the mousse evenly among the molds or pour into the prepared 9- to 10-inch springform pan.

Place the molds in a hot-water bath. Transfer to the oven and bake until the tops have puffed up a bit and appear dry and brownielike, about 35 to 40 minutes for the ring molds and 1 hour for the springform pan.

Set aside to cool to room temperature in the water bath. Remove from the water bath and refrigerate. When fully cooled, remove the plastic wrap and the aluminum foil.

Cover and refrigerate up to 3 days.

Chantilly Cream ✳

*C*hantilly Cream is the fancy French name for sweetened whipped cream. We like Chantilly Cream to be less sweet than most of what you will find; in fact, we often like it with no sugar at all.

2 cups heavy cream
Up to 2 tablespoons sugar
½ teaspoon vanilla extract

Place a large stainless steel bowl in the freezer for at least 20 minutes.

Place the cream, sugar, and vanilla in the bowl and whip with a large whisk until medium peaks form, about 3 to 5 minutes. You can also machine whip for 2 minutes and then whip the rest by hand. Use immediately or cover and refrigerate no more than 3 hours.

TO FINISH AND ASSEMBLE:

1. Using the tip of a paring knife, gently loosen the bottom of the Baked Chocolate Mousse and push up to remove it from the mold.
2. Place each mousse in the middle of a dessert plate and top with 2 dollops of Chantilly Cream.
3. Top with a Chocolate Tuile Fan and toss a bit of broken Crunch around the sides.
4. Serve at room temperature.

SERVES 12

White Chocolate Banana Bread Pudding with Caramel Semi-Freddo and Boozy Caramel Sauce

The back room at Olives is used for private functions and meetings. More often than not, the size of the group grows or shrinks at the last minute. We needed an adaptable fall and winter dessert (ice cream is easy for summer): Our criteria were that it needed to keep for more than one day and be put together with no last-minute fussing. Without any real plan, we made batches and batches of banana bread. But now what? We made banana bread pudding—special but not quite special enough. When we added white chocolate to the custard, we felt that we were getting somewhere, but we still wanted to really wow our guests. A creamy Caramel Semi-Freddo was the perfect answer, especially when complemented by Boozy Caramel Sauce. We cook the sugar a bit longer than usual, giving it a lingering, smoky edge that is not as sweet as most caramels.

Banana Bread ✳

Inspired by a recipe by the mother of Linda Bedrosian, Paige's childhood friend, Paige has reworked the original recipe by reducing the amount of sugar and changing the method. Of course, you can make just the Banana Bread. Make two; it has a way of disappearing.

◆ TOASTING NUTS PREHEAT THE OVEN TO 350 DEGREES. PLACE THE NUTS IN A SINGLE LAYER ON A BAKING SHEET AND BAKE UNTIL LIGHTLY TOASTED, ABOUT 15 TO 20 MINUTES. COOL BEFORE USING. ◆

3 to 4 overripe bananas ("the nastier the better")
1¼ cups sugar
⅓ pound (1⅓ sticks) unsalted butter, melted and slightly cooled
2 large eggs, at room temperature
1 teaspoon vanilla extract
1½ cups all-purpose flour
½ teaspoon salt
1½ teaspoons baking soda
½ cup toasted walnuts (optional) (see box on page 36)

Preheat the oven to 350 degrees. Lightly grease an 8- to 9-inch loaf pan.

Place the bananas and sugar in the bowl of a mixer fitted with a paddle or whisk attachment and whip the bejesus out of them, about 2 to 3 minutes.

Add the butter, eggs, and vanilla, beating well and scraping down the sides after each addition. Add the flour, salt, baking soda, and nuts, if using; mix to combine and scrape down the sides.

Place in the prepared pan and transfer to the oven. Bake until golden brown and firm in the center, about 1 hour. Set aside to cool for 10 to 15 minutes and then invert on a rack.

Wrap and store at room temperature up to 3 days or freeze up to 2 months.

White Chocolate Banana Bread Pudding ✳

*B*anana bread plus white chocolate custard makes banana bread pudding, which can stand alone: no caramel, no semifreddo. It's special enough for even a very significant dinner party. Or better yet, breakfast.

If you have leftover custard or simply want custard rather than bread pudding, you can place the custard mixture in small ovenproof dishes and bake them in a water bath at 325 degrees for about thirty minutes.

2 cups milk
1 cup heavy cream
3 large eggs
2 large egg yolks
½ cup plus 2 tablespoons sugar
½ teaspoon salt
1 teaspoon vanilla extract
12 ounces white chocolate, melted
1 loaf Banana Bread (page 36), cubed (fresh, day old, or frozen)

Preheat the oven to 325 degrees. Lightly grease an 8-inch-square cake pan.

Place the milk and ½ cup of the cream in a saucepan and bring to a boil over medium-high heat. Place the eggs, egg yolks, ½ cup of the sugar, salt, and vanilla in a bowl and gradually add the milk mixture, whisking all the while. Add the melted chocolate and mix until it is fully incorporated.

Place the bread cubes in the prepared pan and pour the custard over it, pressing down to dunk them. Let rest at least 15 minutes and up to 1 hour.

Pour the remaining ½ cup cream over the top and sprinkle with the remaining 2 tablespoons sugar. Place in a hot-water bath and transfer to the oven. Bake until the pudding is firm and a knife inserted comes out clean, about 1 hour.

Serve warm or at room temperature as is, with Boozy Caramel Sauce (page 41), or sweetened whipped cream and sliced bananas.

MAKES 8 TO 10 SERVINGS

Caramel Semi-Freddo ✳

Semifreddo literally means "half frozen"; it's fluffy and aerated, and it has the same mouth feel but is lighter in texture than either ice cream or frozen mousse. It doesn't involve an ice cream machine, just a mixer and your freezer.

3½ cups heavy cream
1½ teaspoons vanilla extract
1¾ cups sugar
½ cup water
½ cup heavy cream
5 large eggs
10 large egg yolks
½ teaspoon salt
¼ cup prepared strong coffee

In a large bowl, whip the cream and the vanilla until it holds stiff peaks. Set aside.

To make the caramel: Place the sugar and water in a saucepan and cook over medium heat until it turns a deep mahogany color, about 4 to 5 minutes. Do not stir. Gently swirl to even out the color. Slowly add the cream and stir very gently. Be careful, it will splatter. Set aside but keep warm.

Place the eggs, egg yolks, salt, and coffee over a hot-water bath and whisk until warmed. Add the caramel and whisk until the mixture is homogenous, thick, light in color, and has the consistency of soft whipped cream, about 4 to 5 minutes.

Immediately pour the mixture into the bowl of a mixer fitted with a whisk and whip on high speed until it cools to room temperature, about 5 to 8 minutes.

Fold in one quarter of the caramel-egg mixture to the reserved whipped cream. Add all the whipped cream to the caramel-egg mixture and gently fold to combine. Pour into a 6- to 8-cup freezer container and freeze at least 4 hours and up to 5 days.

MAKES 1½ TO 2 QUARTS

Boozy Caramel Sauce ✳

*G*reat on any ice cream, drizzled on Pound Cake (page 215), or added to coffee, cappuccino, or milk. You can, if desired, omit the bourbon.

2 cups sugar
½ cup water
½ teaspoon salt
1 cup heavy cream
1 tablespoon vanilla extract
1 tablespoon bourbon

Place the sugar, water, and salt in a small saucepan and bring to a boil over high heat. Cook without stirring until the mixture begins to color, about 4 to 5 minutes. When the mixture is tea-colored, stir lightly with a wooden spoon to even out the coloring. Continue cooking, stirring occasionally, until it turns a dark mahogany color, about 3 to 5 minutes.

Bubbles will rise and when they just start to break up, quickly and carefully drizzle in the cream. It will sputter and splatter and come to a boil at first, but just continue adding the cream slowly and steadily, stirring all the while. Off heat, add the vanilla and bourbon. Set aside to cool to room temperature. Cover and refrigerate at least 2 hours and up to 3 days.

Just before serving, gently reheat over low heat, stirring all the while.

MAKES ABOUT 1 PINT

TO FINISH AND ASSEMBLE:

1. Portion White Chocolate Banana Bread Pudding into 8 to 10 servings and garnish with sliced bananas, if desired.
2. Top with a generous scoop of Caramel Semi-Freddo.
3. Drizzle with Boozy Caramel Sauce.

SERVES 8 TO 10

Milk Chocolate Pot de Crème in a Chocolate Balloon Cup with Hot Chocolate Minis

Although *pot de crème* is referred to as a custard, it is actually a small porcelain pot with a matching lid, which holds the custard. The lid prevents a skin from forming.

Whatever you want to call it or whatever you want to serve it in (and at Olives we don't use a small porcelain pot) we love it. It is a wonderful and mystical thing. Not quite as firm as pudding yet not runny; lighter than crème brûlée and just as satisfying. We played with our original presentation after seeing an old magazine article instructing how to make Easter egg containers out of balloons. The balloon cups are a beautiful and whimsical way to present the sophisticated Pot de Crème and the inevitable irregularities of each only serve to make each shell special. Todd likes it more puddinglike and Paige likes it softer. If you want it stiffer, à la Todd, use another whole egg.

We use only El Rey milk chocolate here. It is less sweet than other varieties and slightly nuttier; it deserves to be shown off.

Milk Chocolate Pot de Crème ✳

8 ounces El Rey milk chocolate
⅓ cup sugar
1 large egg
7 large egg yolks
1 cup milk
1½ cups heavy cream
2 tablespoons liquor, such as Kahlúa or Grand Marnier
1½ teaspoons vanilla extract
¼ teaspoon salt

Preheat the oven to 325 degrees.

Place the chocolate in a small bowl and set aside.

(continued)

Place the sugar, egg, and egg yolks in a small bowl; mix well and set aside.

Place the milk and cream in a heavy-bottomed saucepan and bring to a boil over medium-high heat.

Pour half the milk mixture over the chocolate and stir until smooth. Pour the remaining half over the sugar-egg mixture, whisking all the while, and continue whisking until smooth. Set aside for 5 minutes.

Add the chocolate mixture to the sugar-egg mixture and stir well. Add the liquor, vanilla, and salt and stir well. Pour through a strainer and discard the solids.

Pour into six 8-ounce ramekins or a 1-quart mold and place in a hot-water bath. Bake until the center ripples but does not jiggle, about 30 to 35 minutes for the ramekins and 50 to 55 minutes for the mold.

Allow to cool to room temperature in the water bath, with plastic wrap placed directly on the surface of the custard. Refrigerate until firm and completely chilled, at least 3 hours and up to 3 days.

Old-Fashioned Sour Cream Chocolate Mini Cupcakes *

This beautifully colored cake is an adaptation of a Maida Heatter recipe and a component for the Chocolate Bombe (page 57), but it's a fine cake served any old way. It can be served right out of the oven with heavy cream, with butter (if you're really decadent), or lightly sweetened Chantilly Cream (page 49). This recipe can be halved: Instead of splitting the three eggs in half, use one whole egg and one egg white.

7 ounces bittersweet chocolate
⅜ pound (1½ sticks) unsalted butter
¾ cup sour cream or full-fat plain yogurt
1½ teaspoons baking soda
2½ cups sugar
1 tablespoon vanilla extract
½ teaspoon salt
3 large eggs
3 cups all-purpose flour
1½ cups hot water or prepared coffee

Preheat the oven to 350 degrees. Grease and flour 48 mini muffin cups.

Place the chocolate and butter in a double boiler and cook over medium heat until melted. Set aside.

Place the sour cream and baking soda in a small bowl, mix to combine, and set aside.

Place the sugar, vanilla, salt, and chocolate-butter mixture in the bowl of a mixer fitted with a paddle and mix until just combined. Scrape down the bowl. Add the sour cream mixture and mix until just combined. Scrape down the bowl.

Add the eggs, one at a time, and mix until just combined. Scrape down the bowl. Add 1 cup of flour, ½ cup hot water or prepared coffee; 1 cup flour, ½ cup water; 1 cup flour, and ½ cup water, scraping down the bowl and stirring well after each addition. Do not overmix. Pour into the prepared pan and transfer to the oven. Bake until a toothpick inserted in the center comes out clean and the cake's center springs back when pressed gently, about 16 to 22 minutes.

Serve immediately or cool to room temperature, wrap and store at room temperature up to 3 days or freeze 2 weeks.

MAKES 48 MINI CUPCAKES

Chocolate Balloon Cup

*W*e like semisweet chocolate because its color makes a more dramatic contrast, but you can also use milk chocolate. We don't suggest you use either white or bittersweet chocolate. You can fill these balloon cups with anything soft like pudding, Caramel Semi-Freddo (page 39), or a scoop of Roasted Banana Tiramisu (page 102).

1 pound semisweet chocolate
8 small balloons

Line a baking sheet with parchment paper.

Place the chocolate in the top of a double boiler over low heat and cook until the chocolate is melted. Off heat, stir until smooth.

Blow up the balloons. Holding a balloon by the top knot, dip into the chocolate, rocking back and forth from 12 o'clock to 6 o'clock and then again from 3 o'clock to 9 o'clock, thus forming four petals joined at the base of the balloon. Place the rounded side onto the prepared baking sheet. Repeat with all the balloons. Refrigerate for at least 20 minutes.

When the chocolate has hardened, pop the balloons and quickly remove the deflated balloons from the chocolate cups. Refrigerate until ready to use but no longer than 2 days.

MAKES 8 CUPS

Vanilla Anglaise ✳

*B*asically a vanilla sauce, Vanilla Anglaise is a thick but pourable stirred custard that becomes firm when baked. It is also called crème anglaise.

⅔ cup milk
1⅓ cups heavy cream
1 vanilla bean, split
⅓ cup sugar
4 large egg yolks, at room temperature
Pinch salt
1 teaspoon vanilla extract

Place the milk, cream, and vanilla bean in a small saucepan and bring to a boil over high heat. Off heat, steep for 1 hour.

Remove the bean from the cream mixture, and gently rub the pod to remove the little seeds; return them to the cream. Rinse vanilla bean pod for future use in Vanilla Sugar (see below). Add half of the sugar to the cream mixture and mix well.

◆ VANILLA SUGAR PLACE 4 VANILLA BEAN PODS ON A PAPER TOWEL AND LET SIT AT ROOM TEMPERATURE ABOUT 2 DAYS OR UNTIL THEY ARE BRITTLE. PLACE PODS AND I CUP SUGAR IN THE BOWL OF A FOOD PROCESSOR FITTED WITH A STEEL BLADE AND SPIN FOR 5 MINUTES. SIFT THROUGH A MESH SIEVE TO REMOVE THE POD PIECES. DISCARD THE POD PIECES. ◆

Place the remaining half of the sugar, the egg yolks, and salt in a large bowl and combine well. Bring the cream back to a boil and very quickly pour it into the yolk mixture in a steady stream, whisking all the while. Set aside for 3 minutes. Add the vanilla and stir to combine. Pour through a strainer and discard the solids. Place the mixture in an ice bath and stir until completely chilled, about 20 to 30 minutes.

MAKES ABOUT 3 CUPS

Chantilly Cream ✳

2 cups heavy cream
Up to 2 tablespoons sugar
½ teaspoon vanilla extract

Place a large stainless steel bowl in the freezer for at least 20 minutes.

Place the cream, sugar, and vanilla in the bowl and whip with a large whisk until medium peaks form, about 3 to 5 minutes. You can also machine whip for 2 minutes and then whip the rest by hand. Use immediately or cover and refrigerate no more than 3 hours.

TO FINISH AND ASSEMBLE:

1. Fill Chocolate Balloon Cup with Chocolate Pot de Crème.
2. Top with Chantilly Cream.
3. Drizzle the plate with Vanilla Anglaise.
4. Garnish with Old-Fashioned Sour Cream Chocolate Mini Cupcakes.
5. Garnish with a chocolate tuile twist (see pages 31 and 113).

SERVES 8

Silky Chocolate Cream Pie in an Oatmeal Shortbread Shell

Todd hosted a collaborative dinner with pal and local chef Jasper White, who asked that we make a chocolate cream pie for dessert. Instead of the usual piecrust, we used an oatmeal shortbread crust, and in the chocolate custard, we used the Mercedes of chocolate, Valrhona Manjari. Manjari is a sublime and assertive chocolate, full of depth, fruitiness, and just the right amount of acid. Showcased in the pudding, it doesn't compete for attention but combines well with each element. Once you taste Manjari, you're spoiled beyond repair.

Chocolate Cream Filling ✳

Use the very best chocolate available: This is definitely a case where the quality of chocolate can heighten the experience.

The mixture will seem thin. Don't fret. It should be prepared early in the morning or even the day before, as it takes a bit of time to set up.

¾ cup plus 2 tablespoons sugar
4½ tablespoons cornstarch
Scant ½ teaspoon salt
4½ cups milk
6 large egg yolks
3 tablespoons unsalted butter
1 tablespoon vanilla extract
8 ounces bittersweet chocolate

Place the sugar, cornstarch, and salt in a bowl and mix to combine. Add ¼ cup of the milk and mix until it forms a smooth paste. Add the egg yolks and mix until combined.

(continued)

Place the remaining 4¼ cups milk in a small saucepan and bring to a boil over medium heat. Slowly pour the milk over the egg yolk mixture, whisking all the while. Pour the mixture through a strainer back into the pot, taking care to scrape the sides of the mixing bowl. Discard the solids.

Bring the mixture back to a boil over medium heat, whisking all the while.

Place the butter, vanilla, and chocolate in a mixing bowl and add the hot milk-egg mixture. Set aside for 5 minutes and then stir gently until well combined.

Pour into a shallow 6- to 8-cup container with plastic wrap placed directly on the surface of the custard. Refrigerate at least 8 hours and no more than 2 days.

MAKES 1½ TO 2 QUARTS

Semisweet Chocolate Ganache ✳

*I*f you look up *ganache* in a dictionary, here's your definition: Cooked chocolate and heavy cream that sets into a spreadable icing when it cools.

8 ounces semisweet chocolate
1 cup heavy cream

Method One (to be used when you want to spread the ganache immediately): Place the chocolate in the top of a double boiler and cook until melted. Add the cream and stir until smooth.

Method Two (to be used if you want to pour the ganache immediately): Place the cream in a pan and bring to a boil over high heat. Place the chocolate in a bowl and pour the hot cream over it. Cover for 2 minutes. Whisk until smooth.

Both versions can be covered and refrigerated up to 1 week.

MAKES ABOUT 1¾ CUPS

Oatmeal Shortbread Shell ✳

*T*his melt-in-your-mouth, addictive, divine cookie dough is used here as a pie shell.

When people make these as cookies, the first bite elicits complaints of plainness. Next bite, they can't stop.

½ pound (2 sticks) unsalted butter, at room temperature
½ cup light brown sugar
2 cups old-fashioned rolled oats (not instant)
1 cup all-purpose flour
½ teaspoon baking soda (only use if making cookies)
½ teaspoon salt
½ cup grated semisweet chocolate (optional)

¾ cup Semisweet Chocolate Ganache, melted

Preheat the oven to 350 degrees.

Place the butter and sugar in the bowl of a mixer fitted with a paddle and mix until creamed. Add the oats, flour, baking soda (if using), salt, and chocolate and mix until just combined.

To form tart shells: Cover and refrigerate the dough until firm, about ½ to 1 hour. Dust a work surface with flour. Gently form the dough into 12 flat disks or 1 disk if forming a single 10-inch tart pan; take care not to overwork the dough. Beginning in the middle of the circle, and using short but firm strokes, roll up toward 12 o'clock. Turn clockwise and repeat and continue turning and rolling until the dough is about ½ inch larger than the tart shell. Place the dough in a 10-inch tart pan or twelve 3- to 4-inch ring molds, taking care to lay the dough into the "corners" of the pan, between the sides and the bottom. Gently press into the sides to define the edges. Using your thumb, clean off the edges by pushing the dough against the edge of the pan or mold to cut off excess.

(continued)

Refrigerate for at least 30 minutes or cover and refrigerate up to 3 days. Line the dough with aluminum foil and top with a heavy layer of rice, beans, or pie weights.

Transfer to the oven and bake for 14 minutes. Remove the weights and foil and continue baking until they are lightly browned, about 2 to 3 minutes. Cool to room temperature. Paint the inside with the ganache.

OPTIONAL:

If you would like to make cookies: Place the dough between two sheets of wax paper or parchment paper and roll out to a ¼-inch thickness. Cover and refrigerate until firm, at least ½ hour and up to 3 days. Using a ruler, cut the dough into diamonds and, removing the paper as you go, place on an ungreased baking sheet. Bake until the edges are golden, about 12 to 15 minutes. Cool on the sheet and store in an airtight container for up to 2 weeks.

MAKES ABOUT 4 DOZEN COOKIES

Crunch

*T*he Crunch was added for a texture change and a touch of sweetness.

8 ounces milk chocolate, melted over a hot-water bath and cooled to room temperature
2 cups Chocolate Tuile Fan pieces (page 31) (about 4 ounces); each piece should be about the size of a thumbnail

Line a baking sheet with parchment paper.

Place the chocolate in a mixing bowl and gently fold in the tuile pieces, taking care to coat all the surfaces.

(continued)

Spread the mixture as thinly as possible onto the parchment paper and refrigerate until cooled, about 30 minutes. Break into pieces.

MAKES ABOUT 3 CUPS

Chantilly Cream ✳

*2 cups heavy cream
Up to 2 tablespoons sugar
½ teaspoon vanilla extract*

Place a large stainless steel bowl in the freezer for at least 20 minutes.

Place the cream, sugar, and vanilla in the bowl and whip until medium peaks form, about 3 to 5 minutes. You can also machine whip for 2 minutes and then whip the rest by hand. Use immediately or cover and refrigerate no more than 3 hours.

TO FINISH AND ASSEMBLE:

1. Portion the Chocolate Cream Filling into the Oatmeal Shortbread Shells.
2. Garnish with a dollop of Chantilly Cream.
3. Spear the Chantilly Cream with shards of Crunch.

SERVES 12

Chocolate Bombe with Layers of Smooth, Creamy-Dreamy, Gnarly-Bumpy, and Oh-So Crispy . . .

This dessert is without a doubt the most time consuming and complicated dessert in the book. Make the bombe for a big party when you really want to impress your guests: This is no weekday family dessert.

The concept behind this was to have a self-contained item that would change as you ate it. On the plate, the Chocolate Bombe looks like a whole cake, pretty but no big deal. Then you break it open and voilà: Inside there are more and more layers of every flavor and texture of chocolate.

Chocolate Ice Cream ✳

The one rule about ice cream machines is that they all freeze differently and, as a result, consistency can vary. No matter the machine, Paige and Todd use different basic formulas. While Paige prefers an ice cream with the consistency of soft serve and the ratio of milk to heavy cream to be 3 to 1, Todd prefers that it seem like it just came out of the ice cream maker. He wants a richer product and a 1-to-1 ratio of milk to heavy cream. (For example, for Vanilla Bean Ice Cream [page 112], Todd uses 2 cups each heavy cream and milk: Paige uses 1 cup heavy cream and 3 cups milk. The other ingredients stay the same.) Todd thinks Paige's version feels like ice milk and Paige thinks Todd's version leaves a film in your mouth. Either way, this ice cream is fudgey and dense.

◆ ICE BATHS PLACE A SMALL FLAT-BOTTOMED CONTAINER THAT IS FILLED WITH HOT LIQUID IN A LARGER FLAT-BOTTOMED CONTAINER. SURROUND THE SMALL CONTAINER WITH ICE. SPRINKLE THE ICE WITH SALT AND POUR IN COLD WATER UP TO THE LEVEL OF THE LIQUID YOU ARE TRYING TO COOL. MAKE SURE YOUR CONTAINERS AND THE SURFACE ON WHICH THEY STAND ARE STABLE: WHO WANTS SALTWATER IN HIS DESSERT? ◆

1⅓ cups unsweetened cocoa powder
1 cup sugar
1 cup light brown sugar
¾ teaspoon salt
1½ cups heavy cream
5 cups milk
12 large egg yolks
2 tablespoons vanilla extract

Place the cocoa, sugars, and salt in a bowl and mix well.

Place the cream and milk in a saucepan and bring to a boil over high heat. Add the cocoa mixture to the cream.

Place the egg yolks in a bowl and while pouring the boiling cocoa cream over them, stir slowly. Add the vanilla and strain well. Chill in an ice bath.

Transfer to an ice cream maker and freeze according to the manufacturer's instructions.

MAKES 2 QUARTS

Bittersweet Chocolate Pot de Crème ✳

8 ounces bittersweet chocolate
½ cup sugar
7 large egg yolks
1 cup milk
1½ cups heavy cream
2 tablespoons liquor, such as Kahlúa or Grand Marnier
1½ teaspoons vanilla extract
¼ teaspoon salt

Preheat the oven to 325 degrees.

(continued)

Place the chocolate in a small bowl and set aside.

Place the sugar and egg yolks in a small bowl, mix well, and set aside.

Place the milk and cream in a heavy-bottomed saucepan and bring to a boil over medium-high heat.

Pour half of the milk mixture over the chocolate and stir until smooth. Pour the remaining half over the sugar mixture and whisk until smooth. Set both aside for 5 minutes.

Add the chocolate mixture to the sugar mixture and stir well. Add the liquor, vanilla, and salt and stir well. Pour through a strainer and discard the solids.

Pour into a 1-quart mold and place in a hot-water bath. Bake until the center ripples but does not jiggle, about 50 to 55 minutes.

Allow to cool to room temperature in the water bath, with plastic wrap placed directly on the surface of the custard. Refrigerate until firm and completely cooled, at least 4 hours and up to 3 days.

Old-Fashioned Sour Cream Chocolate Cake ✳

This is the same as the recipe on page 44 but halved.

3½ ounces bittersweet chocolate
6 tablespoons unsalted butter
¼ cup plus 2 tablespoons sour cream or full-fat plain yogurt
¾ teaspoon baking soda
1¼ cups sugar
1½ teaspoons vanilla extract
¼ teaspoon salt
1 large egg
1 large egg white
1½ cups all-purpose flour
¾ cups hot water or prepared coffee

Preheat the oven to 350 degrees. Grease and flour an 8-inch-square cake pan.

Place the chocolate and butter in a double boiler and cook over medium heat until melted. Set aside.

Place the sour cream and baking soda in a small bowl, mix to combine, and set aside.

Place the sugar, vanilla, salt, and chocolate-butter mixture in the bowl of a mixer fitted with a paddle and mix until just combined. Scrape down the bowl. Add the sour cream mixture and mix until just combined. Scrape down the bowl.

Add the egg and egg white and mix until just combined. Scrape down the bowl. Add ½ cup of the flour, ¼ cup of the hot water or prepared coffee; ½ cup of the flour, ¼ cup of the water; ½ cup of the flour, and ¼ cup of the water, scraping down the bowl and stirring well after each addition. Do not overmix. Pour into the prepared pan and transfer to the oven. Bake until a toothpick inserted in the center comes out clean and the cake's center springs back when pressed gently, about 25 to 30 minutes. Serve immediately or wrap and store at room temperature up to 3 days or freeze 2 weeks.

Chocolate Silk

Chocolate Silk is smoother and thinner than fudge but with the same chocolate kick and intensity. We spread it very thin and cut out a small disk; you don't need a whole lot for a mouthful of flavor.

(continued)

2 large eggs
6 tablespoons sugar
10 ounces semisweet chocolate
6 tablespoons unsalted butter, at room temperature
¼ cup heavy cream
1 tablespoon vanilla extract

Line a 18 x 12 x 1-inch baking sheet with parchment paper.

Place the eggs and sugar in the top of a double boiler over medium heat and stir until the sugar has melted. Cover and refrigerate.

Place the chocolate in the top of a double boiler over medium heat and stir until melted. Set aside.

Place the butter in the bowl of a mixer fitted with a whip and beat until creamy. Slowly add the egg mixture in a drizzle. Continue whipping until light and fluffy.

Add the chocolate. Scrape down bowl and add the cream and vanilla. Spread immediately onto the prepared pan. Refrigerate until firm, at least 2 hours and up to 2 days. When ready to assemble, cut into 12 circles with a 3-inch cutter.

MAKES 12 DISKS

Chocolate Crinkle Cookies ✳

¼ pound (1 stick) unsalted butter, at room temperature
4 ounces unsweetened chocolate
2 cups sugar
4 large eggs, at room temperature
2 teaspoons vanilla extract
1½ cups all-purpose flour
½ cup unsweetened cocoa powder
2 teaspoons baking powder
½ teaspoon salt

Preheat the oven to 350 degrees. Line a baking sheet with parchment paper.

Place the butter and chocolate in the top of a double boiler and cook over medium heat until melted. Set aside to cool.

Place the sugar and eggs in a mixing bowl and whip until light and lemon-colored, about 4 to 5 minutes. Add the vanilla and cooled chocolate mixture and mix to combine.

Sift the flour, cocoa powder, baking powder, and salt, add to the sugar-egg mixture and mix to combine. Cover and chill.

Drop by teaspoonfuls on the prepared sheet. Transfer to the oven and bake until soft in the middle, about 10 to 12 minutes. Transfer to a rack to cool.

MAKES 4 TO 5 DOZEN COOKIES

Chocolate Crumb Crust

2½ cups crumbled Chocolate Crinkle Cookies (page 62)
3½ tablespoons unsalted butter, melted
2 tablespoons all-purpose flour
1 large egg white
2 tablespoons chopped semisweet chocolate

Preheat the oven to 350 degrees.

Place the ingredients in a bowl or the bowl of a food processor fitted with a metal blade and process until just combined. Pat into twelve 3-inch ring molds and transfer to the oven. Tamp down the crumb mixture; you just want "bottoms." Bake until dry but still soft, about 12 minutes. Set aside to cool. Store in an airtight container up to 3 days or freeze up to 2 months.

MAKES 12 TART SHELLS

Vanilla Anglaise ✳

⅔ cup whole milk
1⅓ cups heavy cream
1 vanilla bean, split
⅓ cup sugar
4 large egg yolks, at room temperature
Pinch salt
1 teaspoon vanilla extract

Place the milk, cream, and vanilla bean in a small saucepan and bring to a boil over high heat. Off heat, steep for 1 hour.

Remove the bean from the cream mixture, and gently rub the pod to remove the little seeds; return them to the cream. Rinse pod for future use in Vanilla Sugar (page 47). Add half of the sugar to the cream mixture and mix well.

Place the remaining half of the sugar, the egg yolks, and salt in a large bowl and combine well. Bring the cream back to a boil and very quickly pour it into the yolk mixture in a steady stream, whisking all the while. Set aside for 3 minutes. Add the vanilla and stir to combine. Pour through a strainer and discard the solids. Place the mixture in an ice bath and stir until completely chilled, about 20 to 30 minutes.

MAKES ABOUT 3 CUPS

Chocolate Wafers ✳

 thin, crispy, snappy chocolate cookie.

⅜ pound (1½ sticks) unsalted butter, at room temperature
1 cup sugar
1 large egg
1 tablespoon vanilla extract
2 tablespoons prepared coffee, chilled
⅔ cup all-purpose flour
⅓ cup cornstarch
⅓ cup unsweetened cocoa powder
¼ teaspoon salt
½ teaspoon cream of tartar

Preheat the oven to 350 degrees. Line a baking sheet with parchment paper.

Place the butter and sugar in a mixer fitted with a paddle and mix until smooth. Scrape down the bowl and add the egg and vanilla. Add the coffee. Scrape down the bowl and sift the flour, cornstarch, cocoa powder, salt, and cream of tartar into the bowl. Mix until smooth.

Place 1 tablespoon of the dough on the prepared sheet and using the back of a spoon, spread into a thin circle. Continue until the baking sheet is full, leaving 1 inch between each cookie. Transfer to the oven and bake until touching the cookie leaves no wet impression, about 8 to 10 minutes. Let cool on the baking sheet. Transfer to an airtight container for up to 2 days. Can be recrisped if they get soft by placing in a preheated 350-degree oven for 2 minutes.

MAKES 2 DOZEN WAFERS

TO FINISH AND ASSEMBLE:

Confectioners' sugar, for garnish

We use Wilton half-circle domes (6 to a sheet) to make this dessert. You'll need two sets and they are available at JC Penney and most cake-decorating and craft shops. You will also need a 3½- to 4-inch biscuit (not cookie) cutter.

1. Unmold the Old-Fashioned Sour Cream Chocolate Cake. Carefully cut into 3 layers, using a serrated knife.
2. Cut each layer into 4 circles, using a 3½- to 4-inch cutter. (Snack on the trim.) Now you'll have 12 thin circles.
3. Take one circle and place between two sheets of plastic wrap and, using a rolling pin, roll out until the circle is 5 inches across. Repeat with the remaining circles.
4. Remove the top layer of plastic wrap and fit the flattened cake into the Wilton dome; the plastic wrap should be between the mold and the cake. Using your fingers, press the cake in to fit the mold.
5. Fill with about ¼ to ⅓ cup Bittersweet Chocolate Pot de Crème. Smooth the top; the top of the Pot de Crème should be about $^1/_{16}$ inch below the top of the cake.
6. Place the Chocolate Silk circle over the Pot de Crème. The silk should lie flush with the edge of the cake. Cover and refrigerate.
7. Just before serving, drizzle Vanilla Anglaise on a dessert plate.
8. Put the Chocolate Crumb Crust in the center of the dessert plate, on top of the Vanilla Anglaise.
9. Using the tabs of plastic wrap that stick out of the lined domes, pull the dome out and put it in your hand. Pull off the plastic wrap and place the dome on top of the Chocolate Crumb Crust, Chocolate Silk side down.
10. Dust with confectioners' sugar and garnish with Chocolate Wafers and Chocolate Ice Cream.

SERVES 12

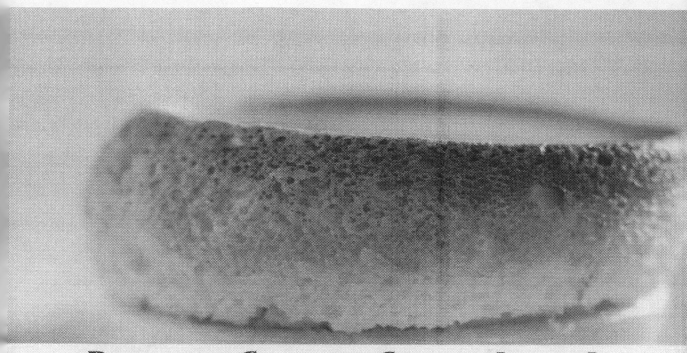

Dreamy, Creamy Custards and Puddings and Tiramisu

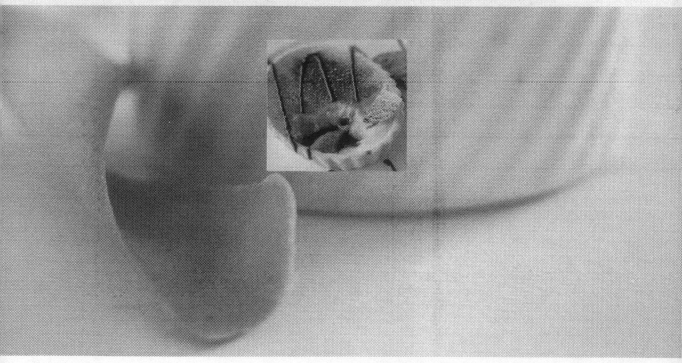

Black-Bottomed Crème Brûlée with Chewy Chocolate Chip Cookies and Chocolate Sauce

Crème brûlée has been popular forever but has enjoyed a renaissance in the past few years. We took the simplest and most elegant of flavors, the oft-maligned but still beautiful vanilla bean, and put chocolate sauce on the bottom, an extra treat you encounter while spooning. The chocolate sauce is gooey when cooled in the custard and is a fabulous foil to the smooth and fragrant vanilla. The chocolate chip cookies add a bit of whimsy: We don't want people to take themselves too seriously.

Chocolate Sauce ✳

Pour this over pound cake or ice cream or mix it into ice cream to make a ripple.

¼ pound (1 stick) unsalted butter
4 ounces semisweet chocolate
2½ tablespoons prepared coffee
2½ tablespoons corn syrup
½ cup sugar
½ cup unsweetened cocoa powder
Pinch salt
½ cup plus 2 tablespoons heavy cream
½ teaspoon vanilla extract

Place the butter and chocolate in the top of a double boiler over medium heat and cook until both have melted. Add the coffee and corn syrup and stir to combine.

Add the sugar, cocoa powder, and salt and stir to combine. Add the cream and stir until all sugar grains have dissolved. Off heat, add the vanilla. Set aside to cool, cover, and refrigerate up to 2 weeks.

MAKES ABOUT 2 CUPS

Vanilla Bean Brûlée ✳

Crème brûlée is said to have originated at Trinity College in Cambridge, England, and is often called Trinity Cream or Burnt Cream because of the process.

We use a blowtorch to brûlée these (Williams-Sonoma carries them). No torch in your kitchen? Fear not: Set your oven to broil and prepare the cooked custards as below, then place under the broiler for a few minutes and broil the sugar! The only drawback to this method is that you need to refrigerate the brûlées for 1 hour after broiling to reset the custard or broil them in a pan of ice water.

2 cups heavy cream
1 vanilla bean, split
⅓ cup sugar (plus extra for sprinkling)
5 large egg yolks
¼ teaspoon salt
2 cups Chocolate Sauce (page 68)

Preheat the oven to 325 degrees.

Place the cream and vanilla bean in a small pot and bring to a boil over medium-high heat. Off heat, steep for 1 hour. Remove the vanilla bean and scrape off any seeds. Rinse the used pod and allow to dry for use in Vanilla Sugar (page 47).

Place the sugar, egg yolks, and salt in the bowl of a mixer fitted with a whisk and mix until the mixture is light in color and the whisk leaves tracks. Reheat the cream over medium heat and bring back to a boil. Pour over the egg mixture in a steady stream, whisking all the while. Pour through the strainer and discard the solids. Cover and refrigerate at least 2 hours and up to 2 days.

Place 1½ to 2 tablespoons Chocolate Sauce in each of eight 5-ounce ramekins. Divide the Vanilla Bean Crème Brûlée among the ramekins. Place the ramekins in a large baking pan and fill halfway with hot water. Transfer the

pan to the oven and bake until the tops quiver but do not ripple, about 50 minutes. Set aside to cool until room temperature. Place plastic wrap directly on the surface and refrigerate at least 2 hours and up to 2 days.

Sprinkle the tops with sugar and caramelize the tops of the custards with a hand-held propane torch set on medium using short sweeping strokes.

VARIATIONS:

Orange Brûlée: Add the zest of 3 oranges to the heavy cream after you take it off the heat. Before straining, add 1 tablespoon chopped orange zest just before pouring into the molds.

White Chocolate Brûlée: Add 12 ounces white chocolate to the hot custard. Omit the vanilla bean. Add 1½ teaspoons vanilla extract and decrease the sugar to ¼ cup.

Chocolate Brûlée: Add 12 ounces semisweet chocolate to the hot custard. Omit the vanilla bean. Add 1½ tablespoons vanilla extract and decrease the sugar to ¼ cup.

Chocolate Chip Cookies ✳

Paige and Todd disagree about nuts. Todd the purist says that nuts should not be in chocolate chip cookies: "They take away from the purity of the whole experience." Paige, a serious nut lover, says that the nuts are essential and that they cannot be optional. "The interruptions of the nut," she says, "make you appreciate the chocolate all the more." You decide.

The colder the dough, the less the cookies will spread and the more cakey they will be. For flatter, crisper cookies, the dough must be at room temperature. These are fabulous frozen, sort of like a candy bar, but beware, if you eat too many, your jaw will ache.

(continued)

¾ pound (3 sticks) unsalted butter, at room temperature
1½ cups light brown sugar
1 tablespoon vanilla extract
2 large eggs, at room temperature
3 cups all-purpose flour
1½ teaspoons baking soda
1 teaspoon salt
24 ounces chocolate chips (2 bags or 4½ cups)
2 cups chopped toasted pecans (see box on page 36)

Preheat the oven to 350 degrees. Line a baking sheet with parchment paper.

Place the butter and sugar in a large mixing bowl and mix until well creamed. Add the vanilla and the eggs, one at a time, and mix to combine. Scrape down the bowl, add the flour, baking soda, and salt and mix until just combined. Add the chocolate chips and nuts and mix until combined. (The batter can be frozen up to 2 months or refrigerated for 3 days at this point.)

Drop by rounded teaspoonfuls (a no. 100 scoop is useful here) onto the baking sheet, transfer to the oven, and bake until the centers are soft to the touch and the edges are slightly golden, about 12 to 14 minutes. Cool on the sheet for about 3 to 4 minutes and then transfer to a cooling a rack. Store in an airtight container at room temperature for 3 days or freeze up to 2 months.

MAKES ABOUT 4 DOZEN COOKIES

TO FINISH AND ASSEMBLE:

1. Place the Vanilla Bean Brûlée on a dessert plate.
2. Drizzle the plate, including the Vanilla Bean Brûlée, with the remaining Chocolate Sauce.
3. Garnish with Chocolate Chip Cookies.

SERVES 8

Ginger Brûlée with Buried Blackberries, Hot and Sassy Cakes, and Blackberry Crush

During berry season last summer we wanted to highlight the gorgeous, showstopping, thimble-sized blackberries we got from Richter's in Washington State (they have obscenely beautiful fruit and every berry is perfect). The fruit was so lush you could crush it to the roof of your mouth with your tongue and feel it explode! We buried a few in the Ginger Brûlée and made a simple Blackberry Crush to give another dimension of fruit. The warm Hot and Sassy Cakes, wickedly spiced baby gingerbread muffins, add a contrast of cool and hot. You decide: What's cool, what's not?

Ginger Brûlée   *

We've jazzed up the classic French custard with a wallop of fresh ginger in addition to vanilla, topped with a brittle layer of sugar. The thickness of the brûlée sugar is a controversial topic. Some like it really thick; we think the sugar should be like the first freeze on a puddle, so thin you can see the custard underneath.

We use a blowtorch to caramelize these, but if you don't have one, they can be prepared as below and broiled for a few minutes to caramelize the sugar! The only drawback to this method is that you need to refrigerate the brûlées for 1 hour after broiling to reset the custard or broil with molds in an ice bath.

2 cups heavy cream
2 ounces sliced fresh gingerroot, about ¼ cup
2 teaspoons vanilla extract
⅓ cup sugar, plus additional for caramelizing
5 large egg yolks
¼ teaspoon salt

Preheat the oven to 325 degrees.

Place the cream and gingerroot in a small pot and bring to a boil over medium-high heat. Off heat, steep for 1 hour.

Place the vanilla, sugar, egg yolks, and salt in a bowl and mix to combine. Reheat the cream over medium heat and bring back to a boil. Pour the cream over the egg mixture in a steady stream, whisking all the while. Pour through a strainer and discard the solids. If desired, cool in an ice bath and refrigerate up to 2 days.

Pour the custard into eight 5-ounce ramekins. Place the ramekins in a large baking pan and fill halfway with hot water. Transfer the pan to the oven and bake until the tops quiver but do not ripple, about 35 minutes if the mixture is hot when put in the oven, or 50 minutes if chilled. Set aside to cool. (You can cover and refrigerate the custards at this point up to 2 days.)

Sprinkle the tops with sugar and caramelize with a hand-held propane torch set on medium using short sweeping strokes.

Serve immediately.

Hot and Sassy Cakes ✳

One guest complained that this was too hot, but be forewarned: If you want just plain ol' gingerbread, don't make this one, make the Apple-Topped Gingerbread (page 211) without the apples instead. Served warm, this cake has buzz, bite, and heat. This can also be made in a 9-inch cake pan.

(continued)

½ teaspoon salt

1½ teaspoons ground cinnamon

2 tablespoons ground ginger

¼ teaspoon ground cloves

½ teaspoon powdered mustard

½ teaspoon black pepper

½ teaspoon white pepper

¼ cup chopped crystallized ginger

¼ pound (1 stick) unsalted butter

¾ cup brown sugar

2 large eggs, at room temperature

⅔ cup molasses

2½ cups all-purpose flour

2 teaspoons baking soda

1 cup boiling water

Preheat the oven to 350 degrees. Grease 24 mini muffin cups.

Place the salt, cinnamon, ginger, cloves, mustard, black pepper, white pepper, and crystallized ginger in the bowl of a mixer fitted with a paddle and mix for 2 minutes. Add the butter and mix until well creamed. Add the brown sugar and mix well. Scrape down the bowl and add the eggs, one at a time, mixing well after each addition. Add the molasses. The mixture may appear broken but just keep going; it will come together.

Place the flour and baking soda in a small bowl and mix to combine. Add half the flour mixture and then ½ cup of the boiling water and combine well. Repeat and mix until well combined. The batter will be quite loose.

Pour into the prepared muffin cups and transfer to the oven. Bake until the top is dry, shiny, and springs back to the touch, about 10 to 15 minutes. Cover and store at room temperature up to 2 days.

MAKES 24 MINI CAKES

Blackberry Crush ✳

*I*t doesn't get any simpler than this: You gently crush and bruise the berries so they make their own juice. The Crush is also great on yogurt, pancakes, sorbet, or ice cream.

2 pints fresh blackberries, rinsed
¼ to ⅓ cup sugar
1 teaspoon fresh lemon juice

Using your hand, gently crush ½ cup of the blackberries. Place the crushed and whole berries, sugar, and lemon juice in a bowl, mix to combine, and refrigerate at least 1 hour and up to 2 days.

MAKES ABOUT 3 CUPS

TO FINISH AND ASSEMBLE:

1. Preheat the oven to 350 degrees. Place Hot and Sassy Cakes in the oven for 4 to 5 minutes.
2. Place the Ginger Brûlée in the center of a dessert plate.
3. Spoon the Blackberry Crush over the brûlée.
4. Garnish with the warmed Hot and Sassy Cakes.

SERVES 8

Pumpkin Ginger Crème Caramel on Spiced Pumpkin Cake with Pecan Shorts and Toffeed Pecans

Pumpkin season, though much anticipated by pumpkin lovers, is very, very short: It has to be cold enough to feel like fall, but the day after Thanksgiving, no one wants to hear about them anymore. Maria Wharton, a member of our pastry team, loves pumpkin and likes heavier spicing than either Paige or Todd, who agree the flavor should be more delicate. Here, a subtly flavored pumpkin custard balances a more aggressively spiced pumpkin cake, accented by buttery cookies and crunchy nuts.

Pumpkin Ginger Crème Caramel   ✳

French custard bathed in caramelized sugar syrup.
Though we usually insist on doing things from scratch, here we use canned pumpkin. It's more consistent, more convenient, and less messy. The flavor and texture of the custard is lighter and creamier than traditional pumpkin pie. If you're serving this on its own, you can make it in a 9-inch pie pan. In that case, bake this custard at 300 degrees for 50 to 60 minutes.

¼ cup chopped fresh gingerroot
1 cup milk
2 cups heavy cream

1 cup sugar
2½ tablespoons water
2 large eggs
½ large egg yolk
1½ cups canned pumpkin purée (not pumpkin pie filling)
¼ teaspoon salt
⅛ teaspoon grated fresh nutmeg

Preheat the oven to 325 degrees.

Place the gingerroot, milk, and cream in a medium saucepan and bring to a boil over medium-high heat. Set aside to steep for 1 hour. Pour through a strainer and discard the gingerroot and other solids.

While the ginger is steeping, prepare the ramekins: Place ½ cup of the sugar and the water in a small saucepan and cook over high heat, stirring occasionally, until the sugar is caramelized, about 8 minutes. Pour into 8 clean, dry 5-ounce ramekins. Tilt the cups so that the bottoms are evenly covered. Set aside.

Place the eggs, egg yolk, pumpkin purée, the remaining ½ cup sugar, salt, and nutmeg in a large bowl and mix to combine. Add the cooled, strained milk and mix to combine. Pour the custard into the prepared molds. Place the molds in a large baking pan and fill halfway with hot water. Transfer the pan to the oven and bake until the custards jiggle but do not ripple, about 30 to 40 minutes. Cool to room temperature and place plastic wrap directly on the surface. Refrigerate at least 12 hours and up to 2 days.

Spiced Pumpkin Cake　✳

*U*sed here as an underliner for the Crème Caramel, it's also a nice tea cake
served alone.

5 tablespoons unsalted butter, at room temperature
¾ cup brown sugar
1 large egg
⅔ cup canned pumpkin purée (not pumpkin pie filling)
¼ cup apple cider
1 cup all-purpose flour
1 teaspoon baking powder
¼ teaspoon baking soda
½ teaspoon salt
1 teaspoon ground cinnamon
1 teaspoon ground ginger
¼ teaspoon ground cloves
¼ teaspoon ground mace
½ cup toasted pecans, roughly chopped (see box on page 36)

Preheat the oven to 350 degrees. Grease and flour an 8-inch-square cake pan.

Place the butter and sugar in the bowl of a mixer fitted with a paddle and beat
until fluffy. Add the egg and beat for 1 minute. Scrape down the sides, add
the pumpkin purée and cider and mix well. It will look broken but don't
worry. Add the remaining ingredients, and mix until just combined. Spread
into the prepared pan and transfer to the oven. Bake until a toothpick
inserted comes out clean, about 20 to 25 minutes. Cool in the pan. Wrap
and store at room temperature up to 2 days.

Pecan Shorts ✳

¼ pound (1 stick) unsalted butter, at room temperature
⅓ cup confectioners' sugar, plus additional for tossing
½ teaspoon salt
1 teaspoon vanilla extract
1 cup all-purpose flour
⅓ cup finely ground toasted pecans (see box on page 36)

Preheat the oven to 350 degrees.

Place the butter and sugar in a bowl and mix until creamy. Add the salt and vanilla and mix to combine. Add the flour and pecans and mix until just combined.

Form a dough into 1-inch balls (a no. 100 scoop is helpful) and place on an ungreased baking sheet. Transfer the sheet to the oven and bake until the bottoms are golden, about 10 to 12 minutes. Cool on the sheet. When they have cooled completely, toss with confectioners' sugar. Store at room temperature up to 2 days.

MAKES 2 TO 3 DOZEN COOKIES

Toffeed Pecans ✳

*M*aking these takes time and effort but it's well worth it. This makes a snappy, salty garnish for crème brûlée or a topping for coffee, caramel, or chocolate ice cream. This recipe makes more than you will need, but since they are so much work to make, we think its best to make a large quantity and keep some in the freezer.

½ pound plus 2 tablespoons (2¼ sticks) unsalted butter
1¾ cups plus 2 tablespoons sugar
1 tablespoon salt
3½ cups pecan halves

Line a baking sheet with parchment paper.

Place the butter in a small saucepan over medium-low heat and cook until melted. Add the sugar and salt and stir briskly until the mixture comes together. Add the nuts and cook, stirring the nuts evenly and constantly, until the sugar caramelizes and coats the nuts, about 5 to 10 minutes.

When the sugar has turned a beautiful oak brown, carefully pour the hot mass onto the prepared sheet and quickly separate the nuts with forks or tongs. When the nuts have cooled completely transfer to an airtight container and store for 3 to 5 days or freeze up to 2 weeks.

MAKES 5 CUPS

TO FINISH AND ASSEMBLE:

1. Cut the Spiced Pumpkin Cake into 9 portions. Eat one and place the remaining 8 on individual dessert plates.
2. Run a paring knife around the edge of each Pumpkin Ginger Crème Caramel and gently push on the edge of the custard to break the vacuum. Tip upside down and center over the pumpkin cake. Allow the crème caramel to drop onto the cake: The sauce will come out of the mold right behind the custard.
3. Divide the Pecan Shorts equally among the plates.
4. Garnish with a handful of Toffeed Pecans.

SERVES 8

Butterscotch Pudding in a Chocolate Crumb Crust with Fudge-Topped Toffee Cookies and Chocolate Lace Cigarettes

We were all raised on boxed pudding mixes and though we may not eat them now, they were our model when we developed Butterscotch Pudding. Our initial forays just did not match up to our childhood memories: The color was too blonde, the texture too pasty, and the flavor too murky. The solution, which took us forever to figure out, was simply to add more salt and vanilla. The bit of caramel matures the flavor and adds depth to the color. This can be made as a nine-inch pie or in twelve individual servings.

Butterscotch Pudding *

Butterscotch pudding is the quintessential comfort food, and this dessert is comfort food at its best, dressed to kill. People so rarely cook for themselves at home and when they do, it's for guests or a holiday. Why wait?

¾ cup cornstarch
6 large eggs
3 large egg yolks
5 cups milk
1⅓ cups light brown sugar
1½ teaspoons salt
¼ pound (1 stick) unsalted butter
2 tablespoons vanilla extract
⅔ cup sugar
⅓ cup water
⅓ cup heavy cream

Place the cornstarch, eggs, and egg yolks in a large mixing bowl and mix to combine. Add ½ cup of the milk and mix until it forms a smooth paste.

(continued)

Place the remaining 4½ cups milk, the brown sugar, and salt in a small saucepan and bring to a boil over medium heat. Slowly pour the milk into the egg mixture, whisking all the while. Pour the mixture through a strainer back into the saucepan, being careful to scrape the bowl clean. Discard the solids.

Return the mixture to the heat and whisk until thickened and boiled, being careful to make contact with the "corners" and bottom of the pot. Transfer to the bowl of a mixer fitted with a paddle. Add the butter and vanilla and mix on low speed until cooled to room temperature, about 20 minutes.

While the pudding is cooling: Place the sugar in a small saucepan. Add the water and swirl gently until it resembles wet sand. Cook over high heat until the sugar starts to color. Do not stir until it begins to color. Gently swirl the pot to distribute the heat evenly and continue cooking until it turns a deep mahogany. Carefully add the cream—it *will* splatter—and slowly stir with a wooden spoon. When the cream is incorporated, add it to the cooling pudding. When cooled to room temperature, pour into a 1½- to 2-quart container. Place a piece of plastic wrap directly on the surface of the pudding, and set aside to cool completely. Cover and refrigerate at least 3 hours and up to 2 days.

MAKES ABOUT 6 CUPS

Chocolate Crumb Crust

2½ cups crumbled Chocolate Crinkle Cookies (page 62)
3½ tablespoons unsalted butter, melted
2 tablespoons all-purpose flour
1 large egg white
2 tablespoons chopped semisweet chocolate

Preheat the oven to 350 degrees.

Place the ingredients in a bowl or the bowl of a food processor fitted with a metal blade and process until just combined. Pat into one 9-inch pie shell or twelve 3-inch ring molds and transfer to the oven. Bake until dry but still soft, about 12 minutes. Set aside to cool. Store in an airtight container up to 3 days or freeze up to 2 months.

Fudge-Topped Toffee Cookies ✳

Almost like a candy bar, these cookies are essentially a soft brown sugar cookie topped with bittersweet chocolate and toasted nuts. Do not use white or milk chocolate.

½ pound (2 sticks) unsalted butter
1 cup light brown sugar
2 large egg yolks
2 cups all-purpose flour
1 teaspoon salt

4 ounces semisweet or bittersweet chocolate, melted
½ cup chopped, toasted pecans (see box on page 36)

Preheat the oven to 350 degrees. Line a baking sheet with parchment paper.

Place the butter and sugar in a bowl and mix until creamed. Add the egg yolks and mix until well incorporated. Add the flour and salt and mix until well combined. Form the dough into a disk and roll out on a lightly floured board and cut with a 2-inch cookie cutter. Place the cookies on the sheet and transfer to the oven. Bake until golden at the edges and medium firm to the touch, about 12 to 15 minutes. Do not remove from the sheet until completely cooled.

Using the back of a spoon, smooth the chocolate in a circular motion onto the cookie almost to the edge and while it is wet, sprinkle with the nuts. Store in an airtight container for up to 2 days or layer between pieces of wax paper and freeze up to 2 months.

MAKES ABOUT 24 COOKIES

Chocolate Lace Cigarettes ✳

These strong yet delicate lace cookies are rolled around a dowel or spoon handle to give them a cigarette-like shape. Their laciness makes them look almost like a stained-glass cookie.

7 tablespoons unsalted butter
½ cup sugar
⅓ cup corn syrup

7 tablespoons all-purpose flour
5 tablespoons unsweetened cocoa powder
Pinch salt
1 teaspoon vanilla extract

Preheat the oven to 350 degrees. Line a baking sheet with parchment paper.

Place the butter, sugar, and corn syrup in a saucepan over low heat and stir until the sugar has dissolved. Off heat, add the flour, cocoa, and salt and stir until smooth. Add the vanilla and stir until smooth. Cover and refrigerate at least 2 hours and up to 2 days.

Divide the dough into 12 pieces and roll each between your wet hands to make thin sausagelike shapes, approximately 6 inches long. Place 6 cookies on the prepared baking sheet, well spaced: They will spread. Transfer to the oven and bake until the shine is slightly dulled and the cookies are dry to the touch, about 14 to 16 minutes. Be very careful when touching the cookies: The hot sugar will stick to you.

Set aside to cool on the baking sheet for 2 minutes. While still warm, pick up the cookies with your hand, one at a time, and roll around a wooden dowel or handle of a wooden spoon. Working with a wet dish towel next to you is helpful: The cookies are not only hot to handle, but buttery and slippery as well. Let the cookies sit seam-side down to cool. If the cookies cool too rapidly and become inflexible, return them to the oven for a minute and then give it another try. If 6 on a pan is too much to handle at one time, try 2 or 3. Set aside to cool and use within 24 hours.

The ends of these can be dipped in melted chocolate for more drama, but it's really the shape and the snap that's a kick.

MAKES 12 COOKIES

TO FINISH AND ASSEMBLE:

1. Spoon Butterscotch Pudding into the Chocolate Crumb Crust.
2. Stick Toffee Cookies into the pudding.
3. Garnish with Chocolate Lace Cigarettes. Sweet chip and dip with an edible bowl!

SERVES 12

Apricot Flan on Sherry-Spiked Marquise with Shortbread Checkerboards and Dried-Apricot Sorbet

What is a marquise? It's not a pâte. It's not a mousse (it has no egg whites). It's more like a bête noire but it has no eggs. It is an intense, solid chunk of chocolate with nowhere to hide.

The original recipe used Valrhona Manjari Bittersweet chocolate with a bit of Grand Marnier. Todd suggested adding a fruity, full Spanish sherry and took the flavor to divine. And then apricot! The intensity of the marquise is tamed by the bite of the tart sorbet and the subtle sweetness and creaminess of the flan.

Sherry-Spiked Marquise ✳

We buy our molds at our most beloved cookware store, Bridge Kitchenware in New York City. A pâté mold is 2½ inches high by 2 inches wide by 12 inches long with a removable bottom and two pins on the side.

This marquise is *soooooo* intense: A little goes a long way.

1 pound Valrhona Manjari Bittersweet chocolate
¼ pound (1 stick) unsalted butter
2 teaspoons chopped orange zest
1 cup heavy cream, whipped
⅓ cup high quality, sweet sherry

Line a terrine with parchment paper.

Place the chocolate and butter in the top of a double boiler and cook until melted. Off heat, add the orange zest and set aside to cool.

Fold in the cream and sherry and spoon into the prepared terrine. Smooth down the top and gently tap the mold to dislodge any air bubbles. Cover and refrigerate for at least 2 to 3 hours and up to 3 days.

(continued)

Using the tip of a paring knife, gently loosen the bottom of the dessert and push up to remove the Marquise from the mold. Allow to come almost to room temperature and remove the parchment. Run a knife under hot water, dry with a towel, and cut into 12 to 16 portions.

Shortbread Checkerboards ✳

These can be time consuming and should be saved for the moments when you are in a perfectionist mood: The more precise you are the more beautiful they are. Don't make these when you're rushed, hungry, or have had too much coffee.

WHITE DOUGH:

¼ pound (1 stick) unsalted butter, at room temperature
⅓ cup confectioners' sugar
1 teaspoon vanilla extract
1 cup plus 2 tablespoons all-purpose flour
½ teaspoon salt

CHOCOLATE DOUGH:

¼ pound (1 stick) unsalted butter, at room temperature
⅓ cup confectioners' sugar
1 teaspoon vanilla extract
⅓ cup unsweetened cocoa powder
⅔ cup plus 2 tablespoons all-purpose flour
½ teaspoon salt

To make the white dough: Place the butter and sugar in a bowl and mix until creamed. Add the vanilla and mix. Add the flour and salt and mix until just combined.

Flatten the dough into a rectangle and place in the center of ¼ sheet (8 x 12 inches) of parchment paper. Top with another ¼ sheet and roll dough to edges of paper.

To make the chocolate dough: Place the butter and sugar in a bowl and mix until creamed. Add the vanilla and mix. Add the cocoa, flour, and salt and mix until just combined.

Flatten the dough into a rectangle and place in the center of ¼ sheet of parchment. Top with another ¼ sheet and roll dough to edges of paper.

Remove top pieces of paper and lay exposed faces onto each other. Brush gently with hands to bond doughs. Using a ruler, cut the dough into fourths, each 2 inches wide (2 x 12 inches). Removing the paper as you go, lay the layered strips on top of each other alternating black, white, black, and so on.

Cover and refrigerate 30 minutes. (Those less precise or simply more impatient may want to slice and bake at this point.) With the side of the slab toward you, using a sharp knife, cut strips of cookies about the thickness of the stripes. Lay the cut striped strips on top of one another taking care to alternate black and white on the outside. Square up the slab, cover, and refrigerate 20 minutes. Cut into ¼-inch slices.

Preheat the oven to 350 degrees. Line a baking sheet with parchment paper.

Place the cookies on the prepared baking sheet, transfer to the oven, and bake until the edges turn golden, about 12 to 15 minutes. Cool on the sheet and remove to a platter. Store in an airtight container up to 2 weeks.

MAKES 3 DOZEN COOKIES

Dried-Apricot Sorbet ✳

½ cup sugar
1 pound dried apricots
3 cups orange juice
½ vanilla bean, split and scraped
2 to 3 cups water
1 to 3 tablespoons fresh lemon juice

Place the sugar and apricots in the bowl of a food processor fitted with a steel blade and process until fine. Transfer to a small saucepan, add the orange juice and vanilla bean, and cook, stirring often, over low heat until most of the juice has been absorbed, about ½ hour. Remove the vanilla bean and save for another use.

Return the mixture to the food processor and process until smooth. Add 2 cups water and 1 tablespoon of the lemon juice. Add more lemon juice and water, in small increments, until it has reached the desired tart/sweetness. Chill in an ice bath. Transfer to an ice cream maker and freeze according to manufacturer's instructions.

MAKES 2½ TO 3 CUPS

Apricot Flan ✳

*I*nspired by the popular Spanish custard, this version incorporates apricot to add lightness. Serve alone with Chantilly Cream (page 35), Vanilla Anglaise (page 47), or a handful of cookies.

You can substitute canned apricots, but they must be packed in their own juices, not in syrup.

10 fresh apricots, pitted
½ cup water
1 cup milk
1 cup heavy cream
1 vanilla bean, split and scraped
6 large eggs
6 large egg yolks
½ cup sugar
¼ teaspoon salt

Preheat the oven to 325 degrees. Lightly grease six 8-ounce ramekins.

Place the apricots in a blender and puree. Strain and discard the solids. Place the apricot purée and water in a medium-size saucepan and bring to a boil over high heat. Lower the heat to low and cook until the mixture has reduced by half, about 20 to 25 minutes. Stir occasionally to prevent sticking. It should yield about 1½ cups purée. Set aside.

Place the milk, cream, and vanilla bean in a saucepan and bring to a boil over medium-high heat. Set aside to steep for 1 hour. Remove the bean, rinse, and allow to dry for future use.

Place the eggs, egg yolks, reserved apricot purée, sugar, and salt in a bowl.

Reheat the milk mixture and bring it to a boil over medium-high heat. Slowly pour the milk mixture over the egg mixture, whisking all the while. Set aside for 5 minutes.

Pour into the prepared ramekins and place in a hot-water bath. Transfer to the oven and bake until it jiggles but does not ripple, about 45 minutes to 1 hour. Set aside to cool in the water bath.

Serve immediately warm or cover and refrigerate up to 2 days.

TO FINISH AND ASSEMBLE:

1. Lay 1 to 2 slices of Sherry-Spiked Marquise on a plate, like shingles.
2. Arrange the Shortbread Checkerboards around the Marquise, leaving one flat.
3. Using the tip of a paring knife, gently loosen the bottom of the Apricot Flan and invert onto the flat cookie.
4. Garnish the Sherry-Spiked Marquise with a scoop of Dried-Apricot Sorbet.

SERVES 6

Banana–White Chocolate Crème Caramel with Brûléed Baby Bananas on a Toffee-Bottomed Cocoa Cake

During the winter it's a challenge to keep the dessert menu fresh when so few ingredients are in season. All-season bananas are so perfectly diverse that we have lots of options. Crème caramel can stand alone, but we wanted more. This dessert is a rarity on Olives' menu: It is a bold, geometric, and architectural black-and-white beauty.

Roasted Red Bananas ✳

You can use regular bananas, but the red ones are sweeter. They can be found in the specialty produce sections of most big-city supermarkets. You can use this as a spread on banana bread or date nut bread.

3 ripe, red bananas
2 tablespoons brown sugar
1 tablespoon dark rum

Preheat the oven to 400 degrees.

Place the bananas in a small baking dish or loaf pan and toss with the sugar and rum. Transfer to the oven and bake until soft and mushy, about 15 minutes. Smash with a fork, stir, and return to the oven for 15 minutes. Smash again and cook for an additional 15 minutes. Set aside to cool.

MAKES ½ CUP

White Chocolate Crème Caramel ✳

This crème caramel is a dessert all by itself. The white chocolate enriches the flavor and gives it more depth than the traditional version.

CARAMEL:

⅓ cup sugar
2 tablespoons water

1¾ cups milk
¼ cup heavy cream
3½ ounces white chocolate
⅓ cup sugar
5 large eggs

Preheat the oven to 325 degrees.

To make the caramel: Place the sugar and water in a small saucepan and cook over high heat, stirring occasionally, until it is a medium caramel, about 4 to 5 minutes. Carefully pour into 6 dry 5-ounce molds. Tilt the cups so that the bottoms are evenly covered. Top cooled caramel with a small dollop of Roasted Red Bananas (page 96). Do not cover the entire surface.

Place the milk and cream in a saucepan and heat very gently over medium-low heat. Place the chocolate in a bowl, pour the milk mixture over it, and stir to melt the chocolate.

Place the sugar and eggs in a bowl and mix to combine. Pour the chocolate milk mixture over the sugar mixture. Strain and discard solids. Pour into the prepared molds.

Place in a hot-water bath, transfer to the oven, and bake until the surface jiggles but does not ripple, about 35 to 40 minutes. Cover surface directly with plastic wrap and refrigerate at least 12 hours and up to 2 days.

Toffee Dough

Rich and buttery, this dough can be difficult to work (it gets soft, sticky, and sloppy quickly), with but it's well worth the trouble.

¼ pound (1 stick) unsalted butter
½ cup light brown sugar
½ teaspoon salt
1 large egg yolk
1 cup all-purpose flour

Preheat the oven to 350 degrees. Grease and flour a 9-inch cake pan.

Place the butter and sugar in a bowl and mix until creamed. Add the salt and egg yolk and mix until well incorporated. Add the flour and mix until just combined.

Pat into the prepared pan and transfer to the oven. Bake until golden at the edges and medium-firm to the touch, about 20 minutes. Set aside to cool.

Top with Kick-Ass Brownie batter (below). Bake until the top is dull and dry but still soft to the touch, about 20 to 25 minutes. Set aside to cool completely.

Draw the tip of a paring knife around the edge of the cookie, tap the bottom, and invert onto a cutting board. Turn face up and cut into 6 portions.

Kick-Ass Brownie   ✻

This is an adaptation of a recipe from Michael Feigenbaum of Lucy's Sweet Endings in Cleveland, Ohio. It is everything a brownie should be: moist, chewy, and kick-ass chocolatey. Use the very best cocoa you can find: We use Valrhona, no question.

¼ pound plus 3 tablespoons (1⅜ sticks) unsalted butter,
   at room temperature
¾ cup sugar
½ cup plus 2 tablespoons light brown sugar
2 large eggs
1½ teaspoons vanilla extract
½ cup plus ⅓ cup unsweetened cocoa powder
⅔ cup cake or all-purpose flour
¼ teaspoon salt
1 cup coarsely chopped toasted pecans (see box on page 36) (optional)

Place the butter and sugars in the bowl of a mixer fitted with a paddle and mix until creamed. Add the eggs, one at a time, beating well after each addition. Add the vanilla and mix to combine.

Sift the cocoa powder, flour, and salt into a bowl and add the nuts. Add half the cocoa mixture to the butter mixture and mix until just combined, scraping down the bowl continuously. Repeat with the remaining half. Spread over cooled, cooked Toffee Dough (page 98).

OPTIONAL:

If you would like to make Kick-Ass Brownies only:

Preheat the oven to 350 degrees. Grease and flour an 8-inch-square cake pan. Spread the batter into the prepared pan and transfer to the oven. Bake until a toothpick inserted comes out dry but with a crumb or two. The top should look dry, craterlike, and crackly, about 25 to 30 minutes. Set aside to cool completely. Cut into 12 pieces. You can trim off all the edges first and then no one has to get an end or an edge (although there are some people for whom this is the best part); crumbled, it makes a great topping for ice cream. Cover and store at room temperature for 2 days or freeze up to 2 months if placed between wax paper and stacked in a resealable plastic bag or a plastic container.

You may substitute chocolate chips for the nuts.

MAKES 12 BROWNIES

Chocolate Sauce ✳

*¼ pound (1 stick) unsalted butter
4 ounces semisweet chocolate
2½ tablespoons prepared coffee
2½ tablespoons corn syrup
½ cup sugar
½ cup unsweetened cocoa powder
Pinch salt
½ cup plus 2 tablespoons heavy cream
½ teaspoon vanilla extract*

Place the butter and chocolate in the top of a double boiler and cook until both have melted. Add the coffee and corn syrup and stir to combine.

Add the sugar, cocoa powder, and salt and stir to combine. Add the cream and stir until all sugar grains have dissolved. Off heat, add the vanilla. Set aside to cool, cover, and refrigerate up to 2 weeks.

MAKES ABOUT 2 CUPS

TO FINISH AND ASSEMBLE:

*6 small red bananas, halved lengthwise
2 tablespoons sugar*

1. Dip cut sides of bananas into sugar.
2. Broil the banana halves, cut-side up, until they are lightly browned, about 3 to 4 minutes.
3. Place one portion of the Toffee-Bottomed Cocoa Cake on a dessert plate.
4. Using the tip of a paring knife, gently loosen the edges of the White Chocolate Crème Caramel. Press on one side to break the vacuum of the custard.

5. Invert and position over the Cocoa Cake. Drop the Crème Caramel onto the cake.
6. Place the broiled banana halves cut-side up next to the wedge of Toffee-Bottomed Cocoa Cake and garnish with a puddle of Chocolate Sauce.

SERVES 6

Roasted Banana Tiramisu

When Todd and Paige brainstorm, Todd inevitably comes up with an idea for a chocolate-banana combo. When he suggested a roasted banana tiramisu, we were inspired! In this updated version of the classic Italian dessert we started with chocolate cake for dramatic contrast, then laced in chocolate ganache and a bit of chocolate mousse. Having so many layers is not absolutely necessary, but the alternating layers of chocolate cake and banana mixture are superb. The coffee syrup cuts the sweetness of the bananas and enhances the chocolate flavor.

The original Tiramisu recipe hails from the Lombardy region of Italy, where mascarpone is the local cheese. Recycling at its finest, it was made of dried, stale cake scraps and probably yesterday's coffee. In spite of the fact that chocolate and banana are, in this case, unorthodox ingredients, we don't care what anyone says: There is no "real" version.

Roasted Red Bananas ✻

You can, of course, substitute regular bananas.

3 ripe, red bananas
2 tablespoons brown sugar
1 tablespoon dark rum

Preheat the oven to 400 degrees.

Place the bananas in a small baking dish or loaf pan and toss with the sugar and rum. Transfer to the oven and bake until soft and mushy, about 15 minutes. Smash with a fork, stir, and return to the oven for 15 minutes. Smash again and cook for an additional 15 minutes. Set aside to cool.

MAKES ½ CUP

Old-Fashioned Sour Cream Chocolate Cake ✳

7 ounces bittersweet chocolate
⅜ pound (1½ sticks) unsalted butter
¾ cup sour cream or full-fat plain yogurt
1½ teaspoons baking soda
2½ cups sugar
1 tablespoon vanilla extract
½ teaspoon salt
3 large eggs
3 cups all-purpose flour
1½ cups hot water or prepared coffee

Preheat the oven to 350 degrees. Grease and flour two 9-inch cake pans or one 12 x 18-inch pan.

Place the chocolate and butter in a double boiler and cook over medium heat until melted. Set aside.

Place the sour cream and baking soda in a small bowl, mix to combine, and set aside.

Place the sugar, vanilla, salt, and chocolate-butter mixture in the bowl of a mixer fitted with a paddle and mix until just combined. Scrape down the bowl. Add the sour cream mixture and mix until just combined. Scrape down the bowl.

Add the eggs, one at a time, and mix until just combined. Scrape down the bowl. Add 1 cup of the flour, ½ cup of the hot water; 1 cup of the flour, ½ cup of the water; and the remaining 1 cup flour and ½ cup water, scraping down the bowl and stirring well after each addition. Do not overmix. Pour into the prepared pan and transfer to the oven. Bake until a toothpick inserted in the center comes out clean and the cake's center springs back when pressed gently, about 25 to 30 minutes. Serve immediately or wrap and store at room temperature up to 3 days or freeze 2 weeks.

Espresso-Rum Soaking Syrup

½ cup brewed espresso
2 tablespoons dark rum, such as Meyer's

Place all ingredients in a bowl and mix to combine. Cover and refrigerate up to 1 week.

MAKES JUST OVER ½ CUP

Chocolate Mousse   ✳

A classic from France, chocolate mousse is a rich, sweet chocolate dessert lightened by whipped cream and/or egg whites. Our version is very, very intense, almost industrial strength. You can pipe it, cut it, or spread it and it still melts in your mouth.

14 ounces semisweet chocolate
3 tablespoons unsalted butter
2 cups heavy cream, chilled
5 large eggs, separated
4 tablespoons honey
⅓ cup sugar

Place the chocolate and butter in the top of a double boiler and cook over medium heat until melted. Set aside to cool slightly; it should be warm, not hot.

Place the cream in a bowl and beat with a mixer or whisk until almost stiff. Set aside.

Place the egg yolks and honey in a large bowl and beat with a mixer or whisk until they reach the ribbon stage: They should be light yellow in color and the whisk should leave quickly dissolving tracks when lifted.

(continued)

Place the egg whites in a bowl and beat with a mixer or whisk until they form medium peaks. Slowly add the sugar and increase the speed to high and whip to stiff but not dry peaks.

When the chocolate and egg yolk mixtures are the same temperature, gently fold the chocolate into the egg yolk mixture.

When the chocolate–egg yolk mixture is just barely warm to the touch, fold in ⅓ of the egg white mixture, ½ of the whipped cream; ⅓ of the egg white mixture, ½ of the whipped cream; and the remaining ⅓ of egg white mixture. Be sure that each addition is incorporated before you add the next one. Transfer to a large serving bowl, cover, and refrigerate at least 3 hours and up to 3 days.

Caution: The use of raw eggs carries the risk of salmonella poisoning. No recipe using uncooked eggs should be served to the very young, the very old, or anyone with a compromised immune system.

Semisweet Chocolate Ganache ✳

8 ounces semisweet chocolate
1 cup heavy cream

Method One (to be used when you want to spread the ganache immediately): Place the chocolate in the top of a double boiler and cook until melted. Add the cream and stir until smooth.

Method Two (to be used if you want to pour the ganache immediately): Place the cream in a pan and bring to a boil over high heat. Place the chocolate in a bowl and pour the hot cream over it. Cover for 2 minutes. Whisk until smooth.

Both versions can be covered and refrigerated up to 1 week.

MAKES ABOUT 1¾ CUPS

Tiramisu Filling

2 large eggs, separated
3 tablespoons sugar
2 tablespoons Kahlúa
2 ounces cream cheese, at room temperature
1 cup Roasted Red Bananas (page 102)
8 ounces mascarpone

Place the yolks, 2 tablespoons of the sugar, and Kahlúa in a large bowl over a hot-water bath and whisk until thickened and fluffy.

Place the cream cheese in the bowl of a mixer fitted with a paddle and combine until creamed. Fold in the banana and mascarpone. Fold into the egg yolk mixture.

Place the egg whites and the remaining 1 tablespoon sugar in a bowl and whip until stiff. Fold into the cream cheese mixture.

Caution: The use of eggs cooked to less than 160 degrees carries the risk of salmonella poisoning. Foods containing these eggs should not be served to the very young, the very old, or anyone with a compromised immune system.

Crunch

8 ounces milk chocolate, melted over a hot-water bath and cooled
    to room temperature
2 cups broken Chocolate Tuile Fans (page 31) (about 4 ounces);
    they should be about the size of a thumbnail

Line a baking sheet with parchment paper.

Place the chocolate in a mixing bowl and gently fold in the tuiles, taking care to coat all the surfaces.

(continued)

Spread the mixture as thinly as possible onto the parchment paper and refrigerate until cooled. Break up the Crunch into shards and use for a garnish.

MAKES ABOUT 3 CUPS

Espresso-Rum Zabaglione ✳

The classic zabaglione is an Italian custardlike dessert, usually made by frothing egg yolks, sugar, and Marsala as they are gently cooked. The French version is called sabayon. Here we've replaced the Marsala with espresso and rum.

This is best served the day it is made. It can be used the second day, but is significantly softer and flatter.

4 large egg yolks
¼ cup sugar
⅛ teaspoon salt
3 tablespoons brewed espresso, at room temperature
3 tablespoons dark rum
½ cup heavy cream, whipped to soft peaks

Place the yolks, sugar, salt, espresso, and rum in the bowl of a mixer placed over a simmering water bath and whisk by hand until lighter in color, slightly thickened, and slightly increased in volume. Place the bowl on the mixer stand and whip on high until the bowl is cooled to the touch. Fold in the cream and serve within 4 hours.

Caution: The use of eggs cooked to less than 160 degrees carries the risk of salmonella poisoning. Foods containing these eggs should not be served to the very young, the very old, or anyone with a compromised immune system.

TO FINISH AND ASSEMBLE:

1. Line twelve 3-inch rings with parchment paper.
2. Cut the Old-Fashioned Sour Cream Chocolate Cake into twelve 3-inch circles.
3. Cut each circle into three layers.
4. Place one layer of cake inside each prepared ring.
5. Brush with Espresso-Rum Soaking Syrup.
6. Spoon melted Semisweet Chocolate Ganache on top.
7. Top with dollop of Chocolate Mousse and spread evenly to edges.
8. Top with dollop of Tiramisu Filling.
9. Repeat once.
10. Top with remaining layers of cake.
11. Brush liberally with Espresso-Rum Soaking Syrup.
12. Cover and refrigerate at least 4 hours and up to 2 days.
13. Just before serving, place the ring in the middle of the plate and remove the ring. Peel off the parchment paper.
14. Spoon the Espresso-Rum Zabaglione onto the edge of the Tiramisu and garnish with shards of Crunch.

SERVES 12

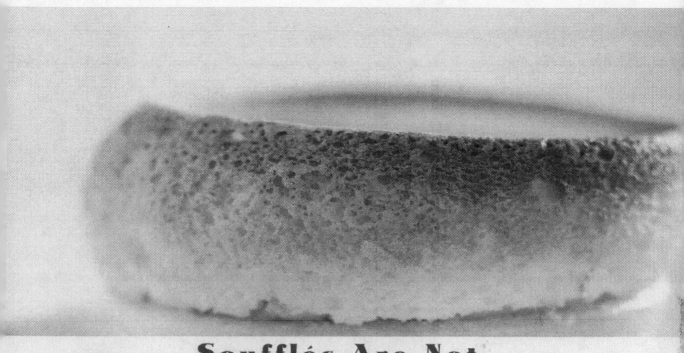

Soufflés Are Not as Tough as You Think

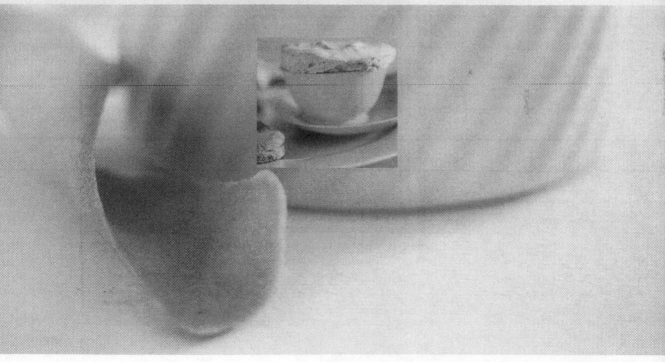

Very Vanilla Bean Soufflé with Vanilla Anglaise, Vanilla Ice Cream, and a Tuile Twist

Todd came up with this vanilla soufflé when Olives first opened and it quickly became one of the most popular desserts on the menu. When Paige arrived, she changed the entire dessert menu. After a few weeks she dropped the soufflé, but the guests went wild: After just three days Olives was inundated with requests for its return. It's an Olives classic and it's here to stay.

In French, *soufflé* means "puffed" or "blown up."

Vanilla Bean Ice Cream ✳

No mere vanilla ice cream, the secret in this beauty is the vanilla sugar. The layering of the vanilla (vanilla bean, vanilla sugar, and vanilla extract) makes it buttery, perfumed, and intense.

3 cups milk
1 cup heavy cream
1 vanilla bean, split
8 large egg yolks
⅔ cup Vanilla Sugar (see box on page 47)
¼ teaspoon salt
1 teaspoon vanilla extract

Place the milk, cream, and vanilla bean in a small pot and bring to a boil over medium-high heat. Set aside to steep for 1 hour. Remove the bean and squeeze out the seeds into the milk. Rinse and dry the vanilla bean pod and set aside for another use.

Place the egg yolks, vanilla sugar, and salt in a mixing bowl and stir to combine. Bring the milk mixture back to a boil and carefully pour the boiling mixture over the yolk mixture, stirring all the while. Off heat, let sit for 5 minutes.

Add the vanilla. Pour through a fine mesh strainer, discard the solids, and chill in an ice bath. Transfer to an ice cream maker and freeze according to manufacturer's instructions.

MAKES 2 QUARTS

Tuile Twist ✳

¼ pound plus 2 tablespoons (1¼ sticks) unsalted butter
1 cup confectioners' sugar
½ cup plus 2 tablespoons sugar
½ teaspoon vanilla extract
½ teaspoon almond extract
¼ teaspoon salt
5 large egg whites
1 cup plus 2 tablespoons all-purpose flour

Preheat the oven to 350 degrees. Line a baking sheet with parchment paper.

Place the butter and sugars in the bowl of a mixer fitted with a paddle and mix until smooth, creamy, and warm, but not hot, about 3 to 4 minutes. Add the vanilla, almond extract, and salt and mix until incorporated.

Add half the egg whites and mix until completely incorporated. Scrape down the bowl, add half the flour, and mix until completely incorporated. Scrape down the bowl and repeat with the remaining egg whites and flour. Cover and refrigerate until spreadable but not liquidy, about 30 minutes.

Place 1 teaspoonful of the mixture on the prepared baking sheet and, using back of a spoon, spread into a 1-inch-wide strip. Place 2 inches apart. Repeat until the baking sheet is full. Return the remaining mixture to the refrigerator.

Transfer the baking sheet to the oven and bake until the cookies are dry to the touch, about 8 minutes. Remove from the oven and immediately, one by

one, twist the still-hot cookie around a wooden spoon handle to form a spiral. Set aside to cool. Repeat with the remaining batter. Cool and place in an airtight container for up to 1 week.

MAKES 24 TO 30 TUILES

Vanilla Anglaise ✳

⅔ cup milk
1⅓ cups heavy cream
1 vanilla bean, split
⅓ cup sugar
4 large egg yolks, at room temperature
Pinch salt
1 teaspoon vanilla extract

Place the milk, cream, and vanilla bean in a small saucepan and bring to a boil over high heat. Off heat, steep for 1 hour.

Remove the bean from the cream mixture, and gently rub the pod to remove the little seeds; return them to the cream. Rinse vanilla bean pod for future use. Add half of the sugar to the cream mixture and mix well.

Place the remaining half of the sugar, the egg yolks, and salt in a large bowl and combine well. Bring the cream back to a boil and very quickly pour it into the yolk mixture in a steady stream, whisking all the while. Set aside for 3 minutes. Add the vanilla and stir to combine. Pour through a strainer and discard the solids. Place the mixture in an ice bath and stir until completely chilled, about 20 to 30 minutes.

MAKES 3 CUPS

Very Vanilla Bean Soufflé ✳

2 cups milk (do not use skim or low-fat milk)
½ vanilla bean, split
¾ cup plus 2 tablespoons all-purpose flour
⅓ cup plus ¼ cup sugar, plus additional for the molds
¼ teaspoon salt
4 large eggs, separated
1 teaspoon vanilla extract
1 large egg white
¼ teaspoon cream of tartar
Confectioners' sugar, for garnish

Place the milk and vanilla bean in a saucepan and bring to a boil over high heat. Set aside to steep for 1 hour. Remove the bean and squeeze out the seeds into the milk. Rinse and dry the vanilla bean pod and set aside for another use.

Place the flour, ⅓ cup of the sugar, and salt in a medium-sized bowl and mix to combine. Add ½ cup of the milk mixture and combine to make a smooth paste. Return the paste to the saucepan with the milk and cook over medium heat, stirring constantly with a whisk, until the mixture just begins to boil, is thick, and has the consistency of oatmeal, about 5 to 8 minutes. Be sure to whisk the bottom and "corners" of the pot. If the mixture gets lumpy, turn off the heat and whisk until it becomes smooth again. Resume cooking over the heat.

Off heat, add the egg yolks and vanilla. Transfer to a medium-sized plastic, glass, or ceramic container and cover the surface directly with plastic wrap. Place in an ice bath. When the mixture has cooled, refrigerate.

One hour before serving, remove the egg yolk mixture from the refrigerator and bring to room temperature.

Preheat the oven to 375 degrees. Butter and sugar six 8-ounce soufflé molds. Be careful to cover the sides all the way up, including the top of the lip.

Place the 5 egg whites and cream of tartar in a bowl and whip with a mixer until the eggs just begin to foam. Gradually add the remaining ¼ cup sugar and slowly increase the speed until it is high; whip until the mixture is stiff and shiny.

Very, very gently fold the whipped whites into the egg yolk mixture, one third at a time.

Divide the mixture among the prepared molds, gently tap on the bottom, and place in the middle of the oven. Bake until the tops are dark gold and the sides are spongelike, about 16 to 20 minutes.

Dust with confectioners' sugar and serve immediately.

TO FINISH AND ASSEMBLE:

1. Place individual Very Vanilla Bean Soufflés on dessert plates.
2. Crack open the top with a spoon and drop in a scoop of Vanilla Bean Ice Cream.
3. Spoon over Vanilla Anglaise.
4. Garnish with a Tuile Twist.

SERVES 6

Double Chocolate Soufflé with Deep, Dark Chocolate Ice Cream, Chocolate-Chocolate Chip Cookies, and Chocolate Anglaise

 hocolate, chocolate, and more chocolate. Serve this to guests and they'll need a designated driver.

Buried Treasure Truffles ✳

8 ounces semisweet chocolate
1 cup heavy cream

Line a baking sheet with parchment paper.

Place the chocolate in a bowl in a hot-water bath and cook until melted, stirring often. Off heat, add cream and whisk until combined. Cover and refrigerate 30 minutes. Using a teaspoon (or a no. 100 scoop), portion into little balls, the size of gumballs. Refrigerate until firm, about 30 minutes. Using your hands, reshape into a round ball. Refrigerate until ready to use or cover and refrigerate up to 1 week.

MAKES 50 TRUFFLES

Deep Chocolate Ice Cream ✳

  1⅓ cups unsweetened cocoa powder
  1 cup sugar
  1 cup light brown sugar
  ¾ teaspoon salt
  1½ cups heavy cream
  5 cups milk
  12 large egg yolks
  2 tablespoons vanilla extract

Place the cocoa, sugars, and salt in a bowl and mix well.

Place the cream and milk in a saucepan and bring to a boil over high heat. Add the cocoa mixture to the cream.

Place the egg yolks in a bowl and pour the boiling cocoa cream over the yolks, whisking all the while. Add the vanilla and mix well. Pour through a strainer and discard the solids. Chill in an ice bath.

Transfer to an ice cream maker and freeze according to the manufacturer's instructions.

MAKES 2 QUARTS

Chocolate-Chocolate Chip Cookies ✳

½ pound (2 sticks) unsalted butter, at room temperature
2 cups light brown sugar, tightly packed
6 ounces unsweetened chocolate, melted and cooled
    to room temperature
4 large eggs, at room temperature
2 teaspoons vanilla extract
½ teaspoon coffee extract (optional)
3 cups all-purpose flour
¼ cup unsweetened cocoa powder
¾ teaspoon baking soda
½ teaspoon salt
24 ounces chocolate chips (about 4½ cups)

Preheat the oven to 350 degrees. Line a baking sheet with parchment paper.

Place the butter and sugar in a large mixing bowl and combine until creamed. Add the melted chocolate. Add the eggs, one at a time, beating well after each addition. Add the vanilla and coffee extract, if using. Add the flour, cocoa, baking soda, and salt and mix until just combined. Add the chocolate chips and mix until just combined. (The dough can be frozen for 2 months or refrigerated for 3 days at this point.)

Drop by rounded teaspoonfuls (or use a no. 70 or no. 40 scoop) onto the prepared baking sheet and bake until the cookies are soft in the middle and have little cracks in the top, about 14 to 15 minutes. Remove from the sheet and let cool on a rack. Store in an airtight container up to 2 days or freeze up to 2 months.

MAKES 48 COOKIES

Chocolate Anglaise ✳

⅔ cup milk
1⅓ cups heavy cream
⅓ cup sugar
4 large egg yolks, at room temperature
Pinch salt
1 teaspoon vanilla extract
2 ounces bittersweet chocolate, chopped

Place the milk, cream, and half of the sugar in a small saucepan.

Place the remaining half of the sugar, the egg yolks, and salt in a large bowl and combine well. Bring the milk mixture to a boil over high heat, and, very quickly, pour it into the yolk mixture in a steady stream, whisking all the while. Set aside for 3 minutes. Add the vanilla and pour through a strainer. Discard the solids. Pour the hot anglaise over the chocolate, stir to combine, and place the mixture in an ice bath and stir occasionally until completely chilled, about 20 to 30 minutes. Cover and refrigerate until ready to serve, up to 2 days.

MAKES 3 CUPS

Chocolate Soufflé ✳

We wrestled long and hard with this classic until it matched Todd's vision of a chocolate soufflé that was more chocolatey than all the others. He knew what he wanted and he didn't care what we had to do to make it work.

The challenge: Using cocoa gives you rich chocolate color but not enough flavor by itself. Add more and you destroy the structure and minimize the essential lightness of a soufflé. Using chocolate is way too heavy on both taste and texture. The solution: Use a bit of both. The result is not as light as the vanilla soufflé, but supreme chocolate flavor with an adult punch from the cocoa.

(continued)

Only make this if you use the absolute best quality cocoa powder you can find!

BASE:

4 cups milk
1 teaspoon salt
1½ cups all-purpose flour
3 tablespoons unsweetened cocoa powder
⅔ cup sugar
4 large egg yolks
2 teaspoons vanilla extract
6 ounces semisweet chocolate, melted

MERINGUE:

5 large egg whites
⅛ teaspoon cream of tartar
¼ cup sugar

To make the base: Place the milk, salt, flour, cocoa powder, and sugar in a small saucepan over medium heat, whisking constantly and taking care to agitate the "corners" of the pot. Continue until mixture thickens and bubbles, about 7 minutes.

Off heat, add the egg yolks, vanilla, and chocolate. Stir well to combine, being careful to get rid of all the lumps.

Pour into a plastic container and place plastic wrap on the surface to prevent a skin from forming. Chill in an ice bath and refrigerate at least 1 hour and up to 2 days.

Allow the base to come to room temperature, about 1 hour, before proceeding with the recipe.

Preheat the oven to 375 degrees. Grease eight 8-ounce molds or one 2-quart soufflé dish. For the 8-ounce molds, place two Buried Treasure Truffles before proceeding. For the 2-quart dish, place 16 truffles.

To make the meringue: Place the egg whites and cream of tartar in a bowl and whip with a mixer until the eggs just begin to foam. Gradually add the sugar and slowly increase the speed until it is high; whip until the mixture is stiff and shiny. Fold a third of the whipped whites into the base; fold in the second and third portions by degrees. Pour into the prepared mold and transfer to the oven. Bake until the tops are dry, about 18 to 20 minutes for the 8 individual molds or 35 minutes for the one large mold.

Serve immediately, no kidding.

TO FINISH AND ASSEMBLE:

FOR INDIVIDUAL SOUFFLÉS:

1. Place the Chocolate Soufflé in the center of the plate and crack open the top with a spoon.
2. Spoon in Deep Chocolate Ice Cream and spoon over Chocolate Anglaise.
3. Garnish with Chocolate–Chocolate Chip Cookies.

FOR ONE LARGE SOUFFLÉ:

1. Crack open the top of the Chocolate Soufflé with a spoon and place a portion of both the crust and interior on each person's plate.
2. Top with a scoop of Deep Chocolate Ice Cream and spoon over Chocolate Anglaise.
3. Garnish with Chocolate–Chocolate Chip Cookies.

SERVES 8

Pumpkin Pie Soufflé with Honey Lace, Cinnamon Anglaise, and Hazelnut-Cranberry Rugelach

Todd wanted an intensely flavored, light, and fluffy pumpkin soufflé, a seemingly impossible task. Our solution was to roast the pumpkin in order to reduce moisture and volume while intensifying the flavor. Still, it was too heavy for our regular soufflé method, so instead we use a more stable, rouxlike base. Eventually, we used the recipe in the Libby's recipe booklet (which you can order using the information on the can itself) for inspiration and enlightenment and went from there. It's been critiqued, mutated, and modified, but we think pumpkin lovers will be happy with the outcome.

Spiced Pumpkin Purée ✳

This purée makes a great smear for toast or even pork chops.

1 can (15 ounces) pumpkin purée (not pumpkin pie filling)
1 teaspoon ground cinnamon
1 teaspoon ground ginger
½ teaspoon ground nutmeg
¼ teaspoon ground cloves
¼ teaspoon salt
½ teaspoon vanilla extract

Preheat the oven to 350 degrees.

Spread the pumpkin purée on a greased baking sheet or shallow baking pan. Transfer to the oven and roast, stirring and smoothing every 15 to 20 minutes, until it loses most of its moisture but is not quite dry and has not crusted, about 30 to 40 minutes. Add the spices, salt, and vanilla and stir to combine. Cover and refrigerate at least 30 minutes and up to 3 days.

MAKES ABOUT 1½ CUPS

Hazelnut-Cranberry Rugelach ✳

Rugelach is a classic and revered horn-shaped Jewish cookie made with a rich and tender cream cheese dough. Here we've enriched it further by substituting hazelnuts for the walnuts and dried cranberries for the raisins.

DOUGH:

½ pound (2 sticks) unsalted butter, at room temperature
8 ounces cream cheese, at room temperature
½ teaspoon salt
2¼ cups all-purpose flour

FILLING:

½ cup sugar
¼ cup light brown sugar
7 tablespoons unsalted butter, melted and cooled
¼ teaspoon salt
¼ teaspoon ground cinnamon
1 cup hazelnuts, toasted and chopped (see box on page 36)
¾ cup dried cranberries, chopped

To make the dough: Place the butter and cream cheese in a bowl and mix, by hand or machine, until just combined. Add the salt and flour, scrape down the bowl, and mix until just combined. (It will be gloppy and soft.) Wrap in plastic wrap and refrigerate overnight.

To make the filling: Place the sugars, butter, salt, cinnamon, hazelnuts, and cranberries in a bowl and mix to combine, making sure the cranberries are well coated.

Preheat the oven to 325 degrees. Line a baking sheet with parchment paper.

To assemble: Divide the dough and the filling into four portions each, keep only one portion out to work on at a time. On a lightly sugared board, roll out one portion to a 7-inch circle, and spread/sprinkle filling over round. Using a large knife or a pizza wheel, cut circle into 8 pie portions. Roll each cut starting at the outside edge and roll up croissant-style. Don't pull too much or it will become too soft to work with; if it does soften too much, refrigerate for 4 to 5 minutes. Place each rugelach on the prepared sheet with the tip tucked underneath the whole cookie. If desired, tuck the "tails" into a crescent shape. Transfer to the oven and bake until the bottoms are colored, about 25 to 30 minutes. Cool on the baking sheet. Store in an airtight container up to 2 days.

MAKES ABOUT 32 COOKIES

Honey Lace Cookies ✳

7 tablespoons unsalted butter
½ cup light brown sugar
⅔ cup honey
¾ cup all-purpose flour
1½ teaspoons ground cinnamon
1 teaspoon ground ginger
Chopped zest of 1 lemon
1½ teaspoons vanilla extract

Preheat the oven to 350 degrees. Line a baking sheet with aluminum foil.

Place the butter in a small saucepan over medium heat and cook until it has melted. Add the sugar and honey and cook over medium heat until the sugar has dissolved.

Off heat, add the flour, cinnamon, ginger, lemon zest, and vanilla and mix to combine. Set aside to cool to room temperature.

Spoon by tablespoonfuls onto the prepared baking sheet. These will spread a great deal so do not cook more than 3 to 4 at a time. Bake until the edges are browned, about 8 to 10 minutes. Let cool on the sheet until cool enough

to remove with a wide metal spatula without tearing, about 2 minutes.
Drape over a rolling pin and cool completely. Store in an airtight container.

MAKES 16 TO 24 COOKIES

Cinnamon Anglaise ✳

*⅔ cup milk
1⅓ cups heavy cream
1 to 2 cinnamon sticks
⅓ cup sugar
4 large egg yolks, at room temperature
Pinch salt
1 teaspoon vanilla extract*

Place the milk, cream, and cinnamon in a small saucepan and bring to a boil over high heat. Remove from the heat and steep for 1 hour.

Remove the cinnamon from the cream mixture, add half of the sugar, and mix well.

Place the remaining half of the sugar, the egg yolks, and salt in a large bowl and combine well. Bring the cream back to a boil and, very quickly, pour it into the egg yolk mixture in a steady stream, whisking all the while. Set aside for 3 minutes. Add the vanilla and pour through a strainer. Discard the solids. Place the mixture in an ice bath and stir occasionally until completely chilled, about 20 to 30 minutes. Refrigerate until ready to use and up to 2 days.

MAKES ABOUT 3 CUPS

Spiced Hazelnuts ✳

*W*hen she was pregnant with their son Simon, Olivia, Todd's wife, was addicted to these.

1½ teaspoons ground cinnamon
1½ tablespoons sugar
Pinch ground cloves
Pinch salt
1 large egg white
¼ teaspoon vanilla extract
3 cups whole hazelnuts

Preheat the oven to 350 degrees. Spray a baking sheet with nonstick cooking spray.

Place the cinnamon, sugar, cloves, and salt in a bowl and stir well. Add the egg white and vanilla and gently whisk to combine. Add the nuts and coat thoroughly.

Spread evenly on the prepared sheet and transfer to the oven. Bake for 15 minutes, tossing nuts every 5 minutes using a metal spatula (like a pancake turner). Set aside to cool. Store in an airtight container for up to 2 weeks.

MAKES ABOUT 3 CUPS

Pumpkin Pie Soufflé Base ✳

*2 cups milk
¼ cup fresh gingerroot, chopped
¼ pound (1 stick) unsalted butter
1 cup all-purpose flour
½ teaspoon salt
1 batch Spiced Pumpkin Purée (page 124)
⅓ cup light brown sugar
½ teaspoon ground cinnamon
¼ teaspoon ground cloves
¼ teaspoon ground nutmeg
9 large eggs, separated
¼ teaspoon cream of tartar
½ cup sugar*

Preheat the oven to 400 degrees. Butter and sugar six 8-ounce molds.

Place the milk and gingerroot in a small saucepan and bring to a boil. Off heat, steep for at least 30 minutes.

While the ginger is steeping, make a roux: Melt the butter over medium heat; add the flour and salt. Mix to combine. Gradually add the milk and cook until thick, about 2 to 3 minutes. Add the pumpkin, brown sugar, and spices and mix to combine. Add the eggs yolks and mix to combine. Place in an ice bath and place plastic wrap directly on the surface. Refrigerate.

Place the 9 egg whites and cream of tartar in a bowl and whip with a mixer until the eggs just begin to foam. Gradually add the sugar and slowly increase the speed until it is high; whip until the mixture is stiff and shiny. Fold the whites into the pumpkin mixture in three stages.

Pour into the prepared molds and transfer to the oven. Bake until the tops are colored and dry to the touch, about 22 to 26 minutes.

Serve immediately.

TO FINISH AND ASSEMBLE:

1. Place the Pumpkin Pie Soufflé in the center of the dessert plate.
2. Spoon Cinnamon Anglaise over the top.
3. Garnish with Honey Lace Cookies and Hazelnut-Cranberry Rugelach.
4. Sprinkle the Spiced Hazelnuts generously over the plate.

SERVES 6

Frozen Citrus "Soufflé" with Lemon Curd and Citrus Shortbread

Even though summer is not citrus season, citrus is a family of flavors that provide refreshment. What's nicer than lemon in summer? Frozen lemon. Although we call this a soufflé, it is really a semi-freddo that looks like a soufflé. It's cool, light, and airy and loaded with flavor. We hid a spoonful of lemon curd inside the mold as a bit of a surprise.

Lemon Curd ✳

There are as many recipes for lemon curd as Carter's has pills. This one is heavy on eggs and egg yolks, which makes it stiffer and more substantial. The butter is optional because, although it adds body and flavor, it isn't essential, just decadent. Use it as a spread for toast or as a filling for cookie sandwiches or a layer cake. Use the egg whites for omelets.

> 4 large eggs
> 15 large egg yolks
> 2¼ cups sugar
> 1½ cups strained fresh lemon juice
> ¼ pound (1 stick) unsalted butter (optional)

Place the eggs, egg yolks, sugar, and lemon juice in a double boiler over low heat and cook until thickened, about 15 minutes. Stir occasionally with a wire whisk to promote even cooking. Raise the heat to medium-high and cook, stirring constantly, until the mixture becomes thickened and tracks form.

Off heat, add the butter, if using, and stir to combine. Pour through a strainer and discard the solids. Cool to room temperature, cover, and refrigerate at least 1 hour and up to 3 days.

MAKES 3 CUPS

Frozen Citrus "Soufflé" ✳

2½ cups heavy cream
½ teaspoon vanilla extract
Chopped zest of 2 lemons
Chopped zest of 2 oranges
3 drops lemon oil

1 cup sugar
¼ cup fresh lemon juice
¼ cup orange juice

4 large egg whites
Pinch cream of tartar
Pinch salt

6 tablespoons orange juice
2 tablespoons fresh lemon juice

8 tablespoons Lemon Curd (page 132)

Prepare eight 5-ounce soufflé molds: Cut parchment strips 1 inch longer than the circumference of the soufflé molds and 3 inches high. Fit around the molds and staple to secure a snug fit.

Place the cream in a mixer fitted with a whisk and beat until medium peaks form. Add the vanilla, lemon and orange zests, and the lemon oil, but do not mix. Transfer to a bowl, cover, and refrigerate until ready to use.

Place the sugar and juices in a small saucepan over medium heat and cook until it reaches the soft ball stage, 236 to 242 degrees (use a candy thermometer).

Meanwhile, place the egg whites, cream of tartar, and salt in a mixer fitted with a whisk and beat until stiff but not dry. Pour the sugar syrup down the sides of the bowl while whipping. Add the juices and whip until cool. Remove the bowl from the mixer and fold in the whipped cream.

Spoon a heaping tablespoon of the mixture into each prepared mold. Tap to settle. Add 1 tablespoon of the Lemon Curd to each mold. Portion the remaining mix into the molds and tap to settle. Smooth the top of molds with the back of a spoon. Cover and freeze at least 4 hours and up to 3 days.

Citrus Shortbread ✳

⅓ cup confectioners' sugar
Chopped zest of 1 lemon
Chopped zest of 1 orange
¼ pound (1 stick) unsalted butter, at room temperature
1 teaspoon vanilla extract
½ teaspoon salt
1 cup plus 2 tablespoons all-purpose flour

Preheat the oven to 350 degrees. Line a baking sheet with parchment paper.

Place the sugar and zests in the bowl of a mixer fitted with a paddle and mix for 3 to 5 minutes. Add the butter and mix until creamed. Scrape down the bowl, add the vanilla, and mix just to combine. Add the salt and flour and mix just to combine.

To roll out into cookies: Form the dough into a disk and roll out to ⅛-inch thickness. Dust off the excess flour and cut into shapes, such as hearts or circles, using a flour-dusted cookie cutter. Using a wide spatula, transfer the shapes to the prepared baking sheet and bake until the edges just begin to color, about 10 to 15 minutes. Set aside to cool on the sheet.

MAKES ABOUT 24 TO 36 COOKIES

TO FINISH AND ASSEMBLE:

1. Remove the parchment paper from the Frozen Citrus "Soufflé" and place soufflé in the middle of a dessert plate.
2. Garnish with the remaining Lemon Curd and Citrus Shortbread.

SERVES 8

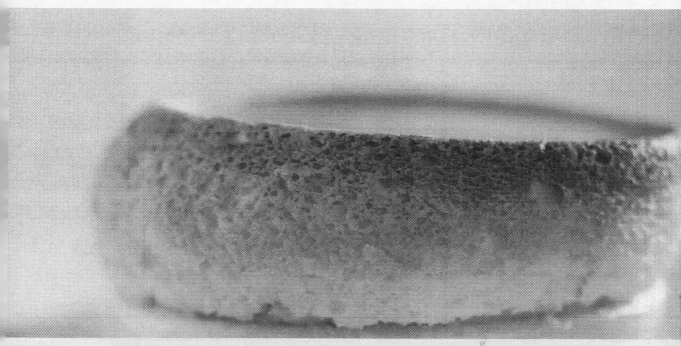

Seasonal Fruits and Tarts

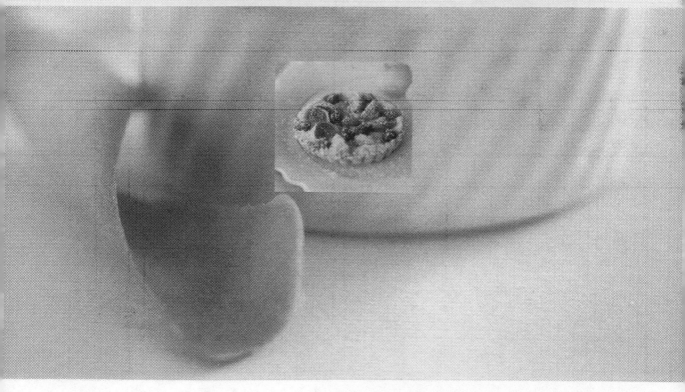

Fresh Fig- and Raspberry-Studded Lemon Tart with Cooling Buttermilk "Ice Cream" and Raspberry Crush

When it comes to figs, there is no middle ground: Either you love them or you hate them. We love them and wanted to show them off in a simple but alluring way. By baking the fresh figs in the lemon custard with the raspberries, we eliminated the often grassy taste and enhanced and showcased the fig itself. The darker fig varieties will "bleed" into the lighter lemon custard, giving it a beautiful blush effect.

Although you can get just about any ingredient any time of year, the best time to make this tart is late summer when you can get the last of the raspberries and the first of the figs.

Pasta Frolla

Pasta Frolla is essentially a more forgiving, more flavorful Italian version of pâte sucrée (a rich sweetened short pastry). However, if not handled with care, it can shrink.

½ cup sugar
Chopped zest of 1 lemon
Chopped zest of 1 orange
2¾ cups all-purpose flour
½ teaspoon salt
7/16 pound (1¾ sticks) unsalted butter, cool but not straight from the fridge
2 large eggs
1 tablespoon vanilla extract

Place the sugar and zests in the bowl of a mixer fitted with a paddle and mix for 3 to 5 minutes. Add the flour and salt and mix to combine. Add the butter and mix until just smaller than pea-size. Add the eggs and vanilla and mix until it is a shaggy mass. Place the mass on a work surface and gather together with your hands, rubbing the board with the mass to pick up the scraps. Pat into a neat and tidy mass, wrap in plastic wrap, and refrigerate for at least 1 hour and up to 3 days or freeze up to 2 months.

Preheat the oven to 375 degrees.

To form tart shells: Dust a work surface with flour. Gently form the dough into 12 flat disks; take care not to overwork the dough. Beginning in the middle of the circle, and using short but firm strokes, roll up toward 12 o'clock. Turn clockwise and repeat and continue turning and rolling until the dough is about ½ inch larger than the tart shell. Place the dough in a 9-inch tart pan or twelve 3-inch molds, taking care to lay the dough into the "corners" of the pan, between the sides and the bottom. Gently press into the sides to define the edges. Using your thumb, clean off the edges by pushing the dough against the edge of the pan or mold to cut off excess.

Line the dough with aluminum foil and top with a heavy layer of rice, beans, or pie weights. Transfer to the oven and bake until the dough is set and dry to the touch, about 10 to 12 minutes. Remove the aluminum foil and bake until golden, about 3 to 4 minutes. Set aside to cool to room temperature.

Fresh Fig- and Raspberry-Studded Tart ✳

This filling is lighter than lemon curd and more custardlike. Although we bake it to temper the grassy taste of the fresh figs, if you don't want to turn on your oven you can simply cool the lemon filling and press in the fruits. Like most fruit tarts, this one is best eaten the day it is made.

1 cup fresh lemon juice
Chopped zest of 3 lemons
Chopped zest of 1 orange
¼ pound plus 3 tablespoons (1⅜ sticks) unsalted butter
1¼ cups sugar

12 large egg yolks
2 tablespoons cornstarch
¼ teaspoon salt
½ teaspoon vanilla extract

One 9-inch parbaked Pasta Frolla shell (or twelve 3-inch shells) (page 138)
1 pint fresh raspberries, rinsed
16 fresh figs, quartered

Preheat the oven to 350 degrees.

Place the lemon juice, lemon and orange zests, 8 tablespoons of the butter, and sugar in a nonreactive saucepan and bring to a boil over medium heat.

Place the egg yolks, cornstarch, salt, and vanilla in a bowl and mix to combine. Pour the lemon mixture over the egg mixture, whisking all the while. Whisk in the remaining 3 tablespoons butter. Pour through a strainer, discard the solids, and set aside to cool.

Pour into the cooled Pasta Frolla shells and arrange the figs, skin-side down, and the raspberries in a concentric pattern (it should look like a sunburst). Transfer to the oven and bake until the fruits just soften, about 12 to 15 minutes. Let cool to room temperature. Best served the day the tarts are made.

Buttermilk "Ice Cream" ✳

Although this frozen dessert has no cream in it, we use it like ice cream. It's not exactly dietetic, but it has substantially fewer calories, less fat, and is more refreshing than its inspiration. We love this served with sliced nectarines and blueberries.

1 cup sugar
12 large egg yolks
2 tablespoons fresh lemon juice
1 quart buttermilk
1 teaspoon vanilla extract

Place the sugar, egg yolks, and lemon juice in the top of a double boiler and cook over medium heat, whisking until it is light and frothy and holds its shape, about 8 minutes. Chill in an ice bath to room temperature.

Off heat, slowly whisk in the buttermilk and vanilla. Cover and refrigerate at least 2 hours and up to 2 days.

Transfer to an ice cream maker and freeze according to the manufacturer's instructions.

MAKES ABOUT 5 CUPS

Raspberry Crush   ✳

2 pints fresh raspberries, rinsed
¼ to ⅓ cup sugar
1 teaspoon fresh lemon juice

Using your hand, gently crush ½ cup of the raspberries. Place the crushed and whole berries, sugar, and lemon juice in a bowl, mix to combine, and refrigerate at least 1 hour and up to 2 days.

MAKES ABOUT 3 CUPS

TO FINISH AND ASSEMBLE:

1. Unmold the Fresh Fig- and Raspberry-Studded Tart and center on the dessert plate.
2. Place a scoop of Buttermilk "Ice Cream" on the tart.
3. Spoon Raspberry Crush on the ice cream, plate, and tart.

SERVES 12

Blueberry-Lime Tart
with Sweet Coconut Crumble
and Blueberry Sorbet

Carla Gracey, a veteran server at Olives, couldn't wait to tell us about a blueberry pie that she'd had at a little bakery in Provincetown. She went on and on and on. From her careful analysis this dessert was born. We ad-libbed a bit and Carla gave it the thumbs-up.

Blueberry Sorbet ✳

Pulpy blueberries are a wonderful fruit to make sorbet with; the result is nothing less than divine. Although *sorbet* is simply sherbet in French, American sherbet usually contains milk, whereas sorbet and European sherbet do not.

3 pints fresh blueberries, rinsed
½ cup sugar
1 tablespoon fresh lemon juice
Splash balsamic vinegar

Place the berries and sugar in a small nonreactive pot over high heat and bring to a boil. Puree and strain. Place the pot over an ice bath.

Add the lemon juice and vinegar. Adjust sweetness with more sugar if necessary. Remember, the sorbet base should be a bit sweeter than you think because the sweetness will be toned down when frozen.

Transfer to an ice cream maker and freeze according to manufacturer's instructions.

MAKES ABOUT 5 CUPS

Pasta Frolla

½ cup sugar
Chopped zest of 1 lemon
Chopped zest of 1 orange
2¾ cups all-purpose flour
½ teaspoon salt
$^7/_{16}$ pound (1¾ sticks) unsalted butter, cool but not straight
   from the fridge
2 large eggs
1 tablespoon vanilla extract

Place the sugar and zests in the bowl of a mixer fitted with a paddle and mix for 3 to 5 minutes. Add the flour and salt and mix to combine. Add the butter and mix until just smaller than pea-size. Add the eggs and vanilla and mix until it is a shaggy mass. Place the mass on a work surface and gather together with your hands, rubbing the board with the mass to pick up the scraps. Pat into a neat and tidy mass, wrap in plastic wrap, and refrigerate for at least 1 hour and up to 3 days or freeze up to 2 months.

Preheat the oven to 375 degrees.

To form tart shells: Dust a work surface with flour. Gently form the dough into 12 flat disks; take care not to overwork the dough. Beginning in the middle of the circle, and using short but firm strokes, roll up toward 12 o'clock. Turn clockwise and repeat and continue turning and rolling until the dough is about ½ inch larger than the tart shell. Place the dough in twelve 3- to 4-inch ring molds, taking care to lay the dough into the "corners" of the pan, between the sides and the bottom. Gently press into the sides to define the edges. Using your thumb, clean off the edges by pushing the dough against the edge of the pan or mold to cut off excess.

Line the dough with aluminum foil and top with a heavy layer of rice, beans, or pie weights. Transfer to the oven and bake until the dough is set and dry to the touch, about 10 to 12 minutes. Remove the aluminum foil and bake until golden, about 3 to 4 minutes. Set aside to cool to room temperature.

Blueberry Filling

> 6 pints fresh blueberries, rinsed
> ½ cup sugar
> 1 tablespoon tapioca flour
> Pinch salt
> 2 teaspoons fresh lemon juice

Place all the ingredients in a medium size bowl, and mix well until about 2 cups of the berries are broken.

MAKES 12 CUPS

Lime Curd   ✳

The butter is optional but not just because it adds calories and fat. The butter firms the curd as it cools and gives it much more body, but it also mutes the zippiness of the lime. The choice is yours. It may also depend on the future use of the curd. Using it as filling? Use butter. Using it for the bottom of a tart? Don't.

> 1 cup sugar
> 2 large eggs
> 6 large egg yolks
> ½ cup fresh lime juice
> ½ cup fresh lemon juice
> 4 tablespoons unsalted butter (optional)
> Chopped zest of 2 limes

Place the sugar, eggs, and egg yolks in a bowl and mix to combine. Add the juices and mix to combine. Place the bowl over a hot-water bath over medium-high heat. Leave a whisk in the bowl and stir every 5 minutes or so, stirring a total of 15 to 20 minutes or until the mixture is thick and begins to leave tracks. Off heat, add the butter, if using, and stir to melt. Pour through a strainer and discard the solids. Add zest and cool to room temperature. Cover and refrigerate at least 1 hour and up to 4 days.

MAKES 1½ CUPS

Sweet Coconut Crumble

1 cup all-purpose flour
2 cups sweetened shredded coconut
6 tablespoons sugar
6 tablespoons light brown sugar
¼ teaspoon salt
7 tablespoons unsalted butter, chilled

Place the flour, coconut, sugars, and salt in the bowl of a mixer fitted with a paddle. Add the butter, a little bit at a time, and mix just until the lumps are pea-size. Use immediately or cover and refrigerate up to 1 week.

MAKES 3½ CUPS

TO FINISH AND ASSEMBLE:

1. Preheat the oven to 350 degrees.
2. Evenly divide the Blueberry Filling among the shells.
3. Top each with a big dollop of Lime Curd.
4. Top generously with Sweet Coconut Crumble.
5. Transfer the shells to the oven and bake until the tops are brown and the filling bubbles, about 30 to 40 minutes. If the topping darkens, cover loosely with aluminum foil and continue to bake until the filling bubbles. Let sit 10 minutes.
6. Carefully unmold into a dish towel that is held in your hand and then invert onto a dessert plate. (Be careful: The juice will be boiling hot.)
7. Garnish with Blueberry Sorbet and the remaining Lime Curd.

SERVES 12

Nectarine-Blueberry Crisp with Oatmeal Crumble and Buttermilk "Ice Cream"

This crisp is a personal favorite of Paige's: The meaty nectarines lend body, the blueberries add a touch of spiciness and jammy sweetness, and the buttery oatmeal crumble offers crunch. What more could she want? Buttermilk ice cream. It's the perfect foil: cool and creamy without overwhelming the fruits.

You can make this in individual ramekins, if you prefer. Bake 20 to 25 minutes.

Buttermilk "Ice Cream" ✳

1 cup sugar
12 large egg yolks
2 tablespoons fresh lemon juice
1 quart buttermilk
1 teaspoon vanilla extract

Place the sugar, egg yolks, and lemon juice in the top of a double boiler and cook over medium heat, whisking until it is light and frothy and holds its shape, about 8 minutes. Chill in an ice bath to room temperature.

Off heat, slowly whisk in the buttermilk and vanilla. Cover and refrigerate at least 2 hours and up to 2 days.

Transfer to an ice cream maker and freeze according to the manufacturer's instructions.

MAKES ABOUT 5 CUPS

Oatmeal Crumble

½ cup light brown sugar
6 tablespoons all-purpose flour
6 tablespoons old-fashioned rolled oats (not quick cooking)
6 tablespoons ground toasted pecans (see box on page 36)
½ teaspoon ground cinnamon
¼ teaspoon salt
4 tablespoons unsalted butter, cold

Preheat the oven to 350 degrees.

Place the sugar, flour, oats, pecans, cinnamon, and salt in a large mixing bowl and toss to combine. Add the butter and cut up with the tines of two forks until the size of a dried pea half. Use immediately or cover and refrigerate up to 24 hours. You may need to loosen the mixture with a fork.

MAKES 2 CUPS

Nectarine Blueberry Filling

2 cups sliced nectarines
1 pint fresh blueberries, rinsed
1 tablespoon all-purpose flour
3 tablespoons sugar
Squeeze lemon juice

Preheat the oven to 350 degrees.

Place the nectarines, blueberries, flour, sugar, and lemon juice in a bowl and toss well. Transfer to a 9-inch pie pan, crock, or casserole and sprinkle with the Oatmeal Crumble. Transfer to the oven and bake until the fruit bubbles, about 30 to 40 minutes.

Serve immediately.

MAKES ABOUT 4 CUPS

TO FINISH AND ASSEMBLE:

1. Spoon the Nectarine Blueberry Crisp into bowls.
2. Garnish with Buttermilk "Ice Cream."

SERVES 6 TO 8

Johnnycake Cobbler with Dark Bing Cherries and Mascarpone Ice Cream

*J*ohnnycake originated in the Rhode Island area and generally refers to cornbread made with white cornmeal. We use yellow cornmeal because it is more readily available.

Almost any fruit is good in a cobbler. We chose dark bing cherries because of their deep flavor; their natural acid cuts the cobbler's bread quality. Instead of putting large drops of dough on the top, we pat out the dough and cut it into little rounds to look like cobblestones, as the name implies. We also offer a raspberry-plum option: Both have strong flavors and contribute different features; the raspberries offer acid, while the plums add sweetness and body. The superb richness of the Mascarpone Ice Cream adds depth and a bit of sin.

Mascarpone Ice Cream ✳

*I*nvented by Mary Copeland, a chef at Ninth Street Grill and the Baricelli Inn in Cleveland.

8 large egg yolks
¾ cup sugar
2¼ cups milk
¾ cup heavy cream
3 tablespoons white rum (we use Bacardi)
½ teaspoon almond extract
1 teaspoon vanilla extract
½ teaspoon salt
1 pound mascarpone

Place the egg yolks and sugar in the bowl of a mixer fitted with a whisk and whip until stiff.

Place the milk and cream in a saucepan and bring to a boil over medium heat.

Pour the hot milk mixture over the egg-sugar mixture, whisking all the while. Add the rum, extracts, and salt and whisk to combine. Chill in an ice bath.

Place the mascarpone in a large bowl and gradually add the sugar-milk mixture. Pour through a strainer and discard the solids. Transfer to an ice cream maker and freeze according to manufacturer's instructions.

Warning: This is higher than normal in fat and should be "underchurned" to discourage butter formation.

MAKES 1 QUART

Johnnycake ✳

We use the sconelike Johnnycake as a topping instead of the more usual crisp or crumble topping. You can also eat it alone as a biscuit.

1½ cups all-purpose flour
¾ cup yellow or white cornmeal
5 tablespoons sugar
1¼ teaspoons baking powder
¾ teaspoon salt
5/16 pound (1¼ sticks) unsalted butter, cold
1 cup plus 2 tablespoons heavy cream

Place the flour, cornmeal, sugar, baking powder, and salt in a bowl and mix to combine. Add the butter and cut in with two knives until the mixture resembles coarse gravel. Add the cream and toss just to combine: It will be a bit sticky. Pat onto a floured board. Using a 1½-inch biscuit cutter, cut out disks and set aside.

MAKES 24 TO 30 BISCUITS

Dark Bing Cherry Filling

9 cups fresh bing cherries, pitted
⅔ cup sugar
Pinch kosher salt
½ teaspoon vanilla extract
3 tablespoons unsalted butter, melted
½ teaspoon ground cinnamon (optional)

Place everything in a bowl and toss together. Use immediately.

MAKES ABOUT 9 CUPS

PLUM-RASPBERRY VARIATION:

Substitute 6 dark plums, cut into eighths, and three ½-pints raspberries for the cherries and increase the sugar to ¾ cup.

TO FINISH AND ASSEMBLE:

1. Preheat the oven to 350 degrees.
2. Divide the Dark Bing Cherry Filling among 8 baking cups/molds or one 2- to 3-quart casserole.
3. Dot with the Johnnycake disks and transfer to the oven. Bake until the mixture bubbles, about 20 to 25 minutes for individual servings and 35 to 40 minutes for a large casserole.
4. Garnish each serving with a scoop of Mascarpone Ice Cream.

SERVES 6 TO 8

Plum Crostada with Mascarpone and Lemon Ice Cream

*I*talian prune plums are so maligned the very word *prune* might as well be a four-letter word. These little oval plums have an olive-type stone, a melonlike green-gold–hued flesh, and a drop-dead gorgeous dusty purple-black exterior. The skin is sour, but when perfectly ripe the inside flesh is jammy sweet. Perfect for the pizza-style crostada, the plums are not overly juicy and don't break down when baked.

Sticking with the Italian theme, we chose mascarpone to cushion the fruit and Lemon Ice Cream just to remind you that you're eating dessert. Without the ice cream this would make a great breakfast.

Yeasted Dough

*T*hese are best served the day they are made, but are fine when reheated for breakfast the next day.

¾ cup milk warmed to 100 degrees
7 tablespoons unsalted butter, melted and cooled
¾ cup sugar
4½ teaspoons active dry yeast
2 large eggs
Chopped zest of 1 lemon
Chopped zest of 1 orange
4¼ cups all-purpose flour
1 teaspoon salt

Place the milk, butter, sugar, yeast, and eggs in the bowl of a mixer fitted with a paddle and stir to combine. Cover and let sit in a warm place for 5 minutes. Change the paddle to a dough hook. Add the zests, flour, and salt and knead until smooth and elastic, about 6 minutes.

(continued)

Cover with a damp dish towel and let sit in a warm place until doubled in bulk, about 1 to 1½ hours.

Divide the dough into 12 portions and place on a floured surface. Shape each into a smooth round ball, cover with a damp towel or a piece of plastic wrap, and allow to double in size, about 30 to 45 minutes. Be sure to space them far apart to allow them to swell in size. Do not let them touch.

Roll the balls on a lightly floured surface into a 7-inch circle. Crimp the edges by placing your left thumb at 12 o'clock naturally on its side, pick up a bit of the edge of the dough just past 12 o'clock and lightly stretch to lay partially over the thumbnail and press down with the right thumb, move the dough a bit counterclockwise. Continue around the tart, lightly stretching and crimping.

Plums and Mascarpone

PLUMS:

36 Italian prune plums, pitted and quartered
½ cup sugar

MASCARPONE:

1 pound mascarpone
2 tablespoons sugar
1 teaspoon vanilla extract

Place the plums and sugar in a bowl, mix to combine, and set aside.

Place the mascarpone, sugar, and vanilla in a bowl, mix to combine, and set aside.

Lemon Ice Cream ✳

The serious lemon aficionado should add 1 cup Lemon Curd (page 132) to the base. If you serve this on its own, try it with Chocolate Crinkle Cookies (page 62) or Pecan Shorts (page 223).

2 cups sugar
½ cup water
Grated zest of 4 lemons
1 cup heavy cream
3 cups milk
8 large egg yolks
1 cup fresh lemon juice

Place 1½ cups of the sugar, the water, and lemon zest in a small saucepan, bring to a boil over high heat, and boil until it reduces to ½ cup, about 5 minutes. Set aside to cool.

Place the cream and milk in a saucepan and bring to a boil over high heat.

Place the egg yolks and the remaining ½ cup sugar in a mixing bowl. Pour the boiling cream over the yolk mixture, whisking all the while. Pour the mixture through a strainer, discard the solids, and add the cooled sugar-lemon syrup. Add the lemon juice and cool in an ice bath.

Transfer to an ice cream maker and freeze according to the manufacturer's instructions.

MAKES ABOUT 1 QUART

TO FINISH AND ASSEMBLE:

1. Preheat the oven to 325 degrees.
2. Spread the mascarpone on the prepared Yeasted Dough tarts.
3. Portion the plums over the mascarpone. Do not go over the folded edge. Transfer the tarts to the oven and bake on the lowest rack until the bottom is toasted and the fruit is bubbling, about 15 to 20 minutes. Serve immediately or cover and store at room temperature up to 24 hours.
4. Garnish with a scoop of Lemon Ice Cream.

SERVES 12

Raspberry Blush Peach Melba
with Almond Madeleines
and Sweet, Toasty Almonds

Peaches are almost decadently beautiful. When freshly blanched and skinned, the blush on the flesh glistens so much it's enough to make you weak in the knees. Why mask such a naturally beautiful sight? Peach Melba is a wonderfully simple, wonderfully flavor-matched treat, rumored to be named after Dame Nellie Melba, an Australian opera singer.

We poach the peaches, plunge them into raspberry purée, and cool them. The surface of the hot peaches absorbs the red color and the raspberry flavor. When sliced, the rosy exterior contrasts with and enhances the orange flesh of the inside. The Almond Madeleines add substance and chew, but are still delicate enough not to overwhelm the fruit flavor. The Sweet, Toasty Almonds add just the right amount of crunch to the plate.

Poached Peaches ✳

When you make this, the peaches should be one day short of being perfectly ripe.

SUGAR SYRUP:

3 cups sugar
3 cups water
½ vanilla bean, split and scraped

12 almost perfectly ripe peaches, halved and pitted but not peeled

To make the sugar syrup: Place the sugar, water, and vanilla bean in a pot and bring to a boil over high heat. Lower to a simmer.

Drop the peach halves into the simmering syrup and cook 5 minutes. Flip over with a rubber spatula and cook 5 minutes. Transfer the peaches to a large

plate and remove and discard the skin. Immediately plunge into the
Raspberry Purée (below). Cover and refrigerate at least 4 hours and up to 2
days.

MAKES 24 PEACH HALVES

Raspberry Purée

Four 10-ounce packages frozen raspberries or 8 half-pints
   fresh raspberries, rinsed
⅔ to ¾ cup sugar
¾ to 1¼ teaspoons fresh lemon juice

Place all ingredients in the bowl of a food processor fitted with a steel blade and
process until smooth. Transfer to a small pot and cook, stirring all the while,
over low heat until the sugar has dissolved, about 5 minutes. Pour through a
strainer and discard the solids. While still warm, add the Poached Peaches
(page 162).

MAKES 4 CUPS

Almond Madeleines　✳

We make these in a madeleine plaque (a pan with individual molds), but
if you don't have one, you can make them in a mini muffin tin, which
will give you slightly less crust.

Chopped zest of 1 lemon
½ cup plus 2 tablespoons sugar
¼ cup confectioners' sugar
7 tablespoons almond paste
2 large eggs
¼ pound plus 1½ tablespoons (1³/₁₆ sticks) unsalted butter,
*   at room temperature, and cut into thirds*
½ teaspoon vanilla extract
1 large egg yolk
1 cup all-purpose flour
¾ teaspoon baking powder
¼ teaspoon salt
¼ cup milk
1 large egg white

Preheat the oven to 375 degrees. Lightly grease and flour a madeleine plaque (this should contain 12 individual molds).

Place the lemon zest, ½ cup of the sugar, and confectioners' sugar in the bowl of a mixer fitted with a paddle and mix for 4 to 5 minutes. Add the almond paste, a little at a time, while mixing. Allow the almond paste to break into pea-sized balls. Add 1 of the eggs and beat until smooth. Add the butter in 3 additions, and mix until light. Add the vanilla, the remaining egg, and the egg yolk and beat until smooth. Add the flour, baking powder, and salt alternately with the milk.

Place the egg white and the remaining 2 tablespoons of the sugar in a bowl and whip together. Gently fold into the lemon mixture.

Pipe or carefully spoon into the prepared molds. Transfer to the oven and bake until the edges are golden, about 8 to 10 minutes. Repeat with the remaining batter. Set aside to cool. Store in an airtight container at room temperature up to 24 hours.

MAKES 36 MADELEINES

Sweet, Toasty Almonds ✳

*G*reat alone as a snack.

1 large egg white
2 tablespoons sugar
Pinch salt
3 cups (about 12 ounces) sliced natural (unblanched) almonds

Preheat the oven to 350 degrees. Spray a baking sheet with nonstick cooking spray.

Place the egg white, sugar, and salt in a bowl and gently whisk to combine. Add the almonds and coat well.

Spread out evenly on the sheet and transfer to the oven. Bake until toasted, about 21 minutes, turning and tossing every 7 minutes. Set aside to cool and store in an airtight container for up to 1 month.

MAKES 3 CUPS

TO FINISH AND ASSEMBLE:

1. Remove the Poached Peaches from the Raspberry Purée. Cut each peach half into thirds.
2. Spoon ¼ cup Raspberry Purée on a dessert plate and arrange three Almond Madeleines on top in a clover pattern, small ends in.
3. Place a cluster of sliced peaches in the middle (the madeleines should be slightly visible).
4. Sprinkle with Sweet, Toasty Almonds.
5. Optional: Serve with Vanilla Bean Ice Cream (page 112) or a high-quality raspberry sorbet.

SERVES 12

Warm Plum Compote over White Chocolate Ice Cream with Peppered-Candied Walnuts and Walnut Biscotti

One day last spring, we'd ordered some great black plums but had no idea what to do with them. Todd's wife, Olivia, came in and excitedly told us about some pepper biscotti she'd just had. We couldn't get the combination out of our minds, and when we started working with the plums, we integrated those biscotti into our recipe.

The slight buzz from the pepper works well with the intensity of the plums and the suave white chocolate smoothes it all out.

White Chocolate Ice Cream ✳

El Rey white chocolate has become an Olives kitchen staple. El Rey treats chocolate like wine: Each harvest produces a slightly different product. Since our menu changes so often, this is not an issue for us. The downside is that the chocolate can be temperamental, and, as a result, needs a bit of TLC. Less sweet than other brands, the vanilla notes make it perfect for ice cream and custards. If you use a brand other than El Rey, such as Valrhona Ivory, reduce the sugar to ½ cup.

3 cups milk
1 cup heavy cream
⅔ cup sugar
8 large egg yolks
½ teaspoon salt
12 ounces white chocolate
2 teaspoons vanilla extract

Place the milk and cream in a saucepan and bring to a boil over high heat. Place the sugar, egg yolks, and salt in a bowl and stir to combine. Pour the hot

milk mixture over the sugar mixture, whisking all the while. Add the white chocolate and allow to sit for 5 minutes. Stir to combine, pour through a strainer, and discard the solids. Add the vanilla.

Chill in an ice bath. Transfer to an ice cream maker and freeze according to the manufacturer's instructions.

MAKES ABOUT 1 QUART

Peppered Walnut Biscotti ✳

*D*epending on who slices them, these biscotti turn out very differently: Todd likes them long and paper-thin, Paige squat and fat.

¼ pound (1 stick) unsalted butter, at room temperature
¾ cup sugar
¼ cup brown sugar
2 large eggs
1 tablespoon vanilla extract
2¼ cups all-purpose flour
½ cup toasted walnuts, ground (see box on page 36)
1½ teaspoons baking powder
1 teaspoon ground black pepper
½ teaspoon salt
1½ cups lightly toasted walnut pieces (see box on page 36)

Line a baking sheet with parchment paper.

Place the butter and sugars in the bowl of a mixer fitted with a paddle and mix until light and fluffy. Add the eggs, one at a time, scraping down the bowl after each addition. Add the vanilla and mix.

Place the flour, ground walnuts, baking powder, pepper, and salt in a bowl and toss to combine. Add the dry ingredients to the butter mixture and mix on low until almost combine. Scrape down the sides, add the walnut pieces, and mix until just combined.

On a lightly floured board, divide the dough in half and roll into two 12-inch logs. Place the logs about 4 inches apart on the prepared pan and refrigerate for 20 minutes. Take care not to have gross creases in the dough as these will become fissures as the cookies bake.

Preheat the oven to 325 degrees.

Transfer the pan to the oven and bake until the tops crack and the center is firm to the touch, about 25 to 30 minutes. Allow to cool on the pans. If desired, the log(s) can be wrapped and frozen for future use.

Cut the logs on a diagonal. For long, severely diagonal cookies, slice very thin, about ⅛-inch thickness. For a squat, fat cookie; slice on a slight slant and cut to ½- to 1-inch thickness.

Preheat the oven to 250 degrees. Line a baking sheet with parchment paper.

Place the cookies on the baking sheet and transfer to the oven. Bake until lightly toasted, about 12 to 15 minutes for the thinner ones, about 15 to 18 for the thicker ones. Cool on the sheet but be aware, the cookies will continue to dry even as they cool. Store in an airtight container up to 3 weeks. If these soften, they can be recrisped in a 300-degree oven for 2 to 3 minutes.

MAKES 36 TO 60 COOKIES, DEPENDING ON HOW YOU SLICE THEM

Peppered-Candied Walnuts *

*H*ot and sweet, these also make a great cocktail snack.

¾ cup plus 2 tablespoons sugar
2 tablespoons unsalted butter
2 cups walnut pieces
1 teaspoon salt
½ teaspoon ground cumin
1 teaspoon ground black pepper
¼ teaspoon cayenne

Preheat the oven to 350 degrees.

Place ¾ cup of the sugar in a small skillet over high heat and cook until it turns a light caramel color, about 4 to 5 minutes. Stir to even out the color. Add the butter and stir to combine. Add the nuts and stir to coat.

Spread on a baking sheet and transfer to the oven. Bake until the nuts are toasted, about 15 minutes, turning and tossing every 5 minutes.

Pour the nuts into a mixing bowl, add the salt and spices and the remaining 2 tablespoons sugar and very quickly toss the nuts (like flipping pancakes) repeatedly to coat them evenly. Immediately spread onto a piece of parchment paper and separate with a fork to cool. Allow to cool completely. Store in an airtight container up to 1 month.

MAKES ABOUT 2½ CUPS

Plum Compote

15 ripe, dark red plums (about 3 pounds), cut into eighths
½ to ¾ cup sugar
Fresh lemon juice

Place the plums and ½ cup of the sugar in a small pot and set aside for 20 minutes. Transfer to the stove and cook, stirring constantly, over medium heat until the plums soften and just start to lose their clean edges, about 5 to 7 minutes. Set aside to cool and add more sugar if desired and lemon juice to taste.

MAKES 4 CUPS

TO FINISH AND ASSEMBLE:

1. Place the White Chocolate Ice Cream in a dish and spoon warm Plum Compote over it.
2. Garnish with Peppered Walnut Biscotti and Peppered-Candied Walnuts.

SERVES 4

Apricot and Goat Cheese Tart in a Pistachio Shell

*T*his is an intriguing dessert item that is more savory than sweet; the fruit is relatively unadorned and there's very little sugar. The goat cheese heightens the clean citrus tang of the apricots, but also showcases the sweetness of the fruit. The pistachios add an additional dimension of texture and earthy flavor without detracting from the other elements. This can be served hot or at room temperature, for dessert or as a damn good breakfast.

Pistachio Tart Shell

*J*ust a basic tart dough with ground-up pistachios.

½ cup finely ground pistachio nuts
½ cup sugar
2½ cups all-purpose flour
½ teaspoon salt
⅜ pound (1½ sticks) unsalted butter, chilled
Chopped zest of 1 lemon
2 large eggs
1 tablespoon vanilla extract

Lightly flour a work surface.

Place the nuts and sugar in a food processor fitted with a steel blade and process until fine. Add the flour, salt, and butter and pulse until sandy. Add the zest, eggs, and vanilla and pulse until it forms a shaggy mass.

Place the dough on the work surface and gather into a cohesive mass. Cover with plastic wrap and refrigerate at least 1 hour and up to 2 days. Divide into eight portions.

To form tart shells: Dust a work surface with flour. Gently form the dough into 8 flat disks; take care not to overwork the dough. Beginning in the middle of

the circle, and using short but firm strokes, roll up toward 12 o'clock. Turn clockwise and repeat and continue turning and rolling until the dough is about ½ inch larger than the tart shell. Place the dough in eight 4-inch tart pans, taking care to lay the dough into the "corners" of the pan, between the sides and the bottom. Gently press into the sides to define the edges. Using your thumb, clean off the edges by pushing the dough against the edge of the pan or mold to cut off excess.

Line the dough with aluminum foil and top with a heavy layer of rice, beans, or pie weights. Transfer to the oven and bake until the dough is set and dry to the touch, about 10 to 12 minutes. Remove the aluminum foil and bake until golden, about 3 to 4 minutes. Set aside to cool to room temperature.

Apricot and Goat Cheese

16 ripe apricots, pitted and quartered
⅓ cup sugar
1 tablespoon fresh lemon juice

8 ounces goat cheese
½ cup toasted pistachios (see box on page 36)

Preheat the oven to 350 degrees.

Place the apricots, sugar, and lemon juice in a bowl and toss well.

TO FINISH AND ASSEMBLE:

1. Dot the pistachio Tart Shells with equal amounts of half of the goat cheese.
2. Top with pistachios, the apricots, and then dot again with the remaining half of the goat cheese.
3. Transfer to the oven and bake until golden and bubbly, about 20 to 25 minutes.
4. Serve warm or at room temperature.

SERVES 8

Chocolate-Laced Caramelized Hazelnut Tart with Chocolate Semi-Freddo and Hazelnut Sandwich Cookies

Hazelnuts are most gorgeous when left whole. Could our guests, we asked ourselves, accept a whole mouthful of just hazelnuts? Definitely! The pastry shell is shallow and small but the flavor packs a punch. It's filled with nothing but roasted hazelnuts and just enough dark caramel to hold them together. The Chocolate Semi-Freddo tempers the nuts. The Hazelnut Sandwich Cookies and Chocolate Drizzle complete this dessert perfectly. It's a beauty.

Caramel Sauce ✳

> 2 cups sugar
> ½ cup water
> ½ teaspoon salt
> 1 cup heavy cream
> 1 tablespoon vanilla extract
> 1 tablespoon bourbon

Place the sugar, water, and salt in a small saucepan and bring to a boil over high heat. Cook without stirring until the mixture begins to color, about 4 to 5 minutes. When the mixture is tea-colored, stir lightly with a wooden spoon to even out the coloring. Continue cooking over high heat, stirring occasionally, until it turns a dark mahogany color, about 3 to 5 minutes.

Bubbles will rise and when they just start to break up, quickly and carefully drizzle in the cream. It will sputter and splatter and come to a boil at first, but just continue adding the cream slowly and steadily, stirring all the while. Off heat, add the vanilla and bourbon. Set aside to cool to room temperature. Cover and refrigerate at least 2 hours and up to 3 days.

Just before serving, gently reheat over low heat, stirring all the while.

MAKES ABOUT 1 PINT

Chocolate Semi-Freddo ✳

The mousselike texture of the of the semifreddo is best right after it's made. After freezing it will be more like a light ice cream.

2 cups heavy cream
2 tablespoons Kahlúa
1⅓ cups sugar
1 tablespoon light corn syrup
½ cup water
5 large egg whites
¼ teaspoon salt
10 ounces El Rey or Callebaut bittersweet chocolate, melted
   and cooled to room temperature
4 tablespoons unsalted butter, melted and cooled to room temperature

Place the cream and Kahlúa in a mixer fitted with a whisk and whip until it is stiff enough to just hold its shape. Cover and refrigerate.

Place the sugar and corn syrup in a small saucepan and gradually add the water until it looks like wet sand. Cook over medium-high heat until it reaches the soft ball stage, 234 to 240 degrees, being sure to wash down any crystals that form on the sides of the pot. (An easy method to remove crystals is to place a small bowl over the opening of the pot. The condensation will be trapped and run down the sides of the pot, washing down any sugar crystals.)

Place the egg whites in a mixer fitted with a whisk and whip until stiff peaks form, about 4 to 5 minutes. Add the salt. Pour the cooked sugar down the inside of the bowl (and not directly into the mixture) and continue whipping until the bowl is room temperature.

Fold the melted chocolate and butter into the whipped egg white mixture. Fold in the whipped cream.

Pour into a plastic container and freeze at least 4 hours and up to 1 week.

MAKES ABOUT 2 QUARTS

Pasta Frolla

½ cup sugar
Chopped zest of 1 lemon
Chopped zest of 1 orange
2¾ cups all-purpose flour
½ teaspoon salt
⁷⁄₁₆ pound (1¾ sticks) unsalted butter, cool but not straight
    from the fridge
2 large eggs
1 tablespoon vanilla extract

Place the sugar and zests in the bowl of a mixer fitted with a paddle and mix for 3 to 5 minutes. Add the flour and salt and mix to combine. Add the butter and mix until just smaller than pea-size. Add the egg and vanilla and mix until it is a shaggy mass. Place the mass on a lightly floured work surface and gather together with your hands, rubbing the board with the mass to pick up the scraps. Pat into a neat and tidy mass, wrap in plastic wrap, and refrigerate for at least 1 hour and up to 3 days or freeze up to 2 months.

Preheat the oven to 375 degrees.

To form tart shells: Dust a work surface with flour. Gently form the dough into 12 flat disks; take care not to overwork the dough. Beginning in the middle of the circle, and using short but firm strokes, roll up toward 12 o'clock. Turn clockwise and repeat and continue turning and rolling until the dough is about ½ inch larger than the tart shell. Place the dough in twelve 3-inch tart pans or molds, taking care to lay the dough into the "corners" of the pan, between the sides and the bottom. Gently press into the sides to define the edges. Using your thumb, clean off the edges by pushing the dough against the edge of the pan or mold to cut off excess.

Line the dough with aluminum foil and top with a heavy layer of rice, beans, or pie weights. Transfer to the oven and bake until the dough is set and dry to the touch, about 10 to 12 minutes. Remove the aluminum foil and bake until golden, about 3 to 4 minutes. Set aside to cool to room temperature.

Caramelized Hazelnut Tart ✳

These hold extremely well for three days covered at room temperature, but any longer and the shell loses its personality.

For a nice change, make the Pasta Frolla shell, substituting ¾ cup unsweetened cocoa for ¾ cup flour, and serve with Deep Chocolate Ice Cream (page 119).

1½ cups sugar
¾ cup water
1 cup plus 2 tablespoons heavy cream
6 cups hazelnuts (or 4½ cups sliced almonds, 6 cups walnuts, or
    5¼ cups whole almonds)
3 ounces milk chocolate, melted
Twelve 3-inch parbaked Pasta Frolla shells, in their molds (page 178)

Preheat the oven to 325 degrees.

Place the sugar and water in a pot and bring to a boil over high heat. Cook, stirring occasionally, until it is a light caramel color, about 5 minutes. Gradually add the cream, stirring all the while, and cook until it boils; watch out for splattering. Add the nuts and stir to coat.

Spoon into twelve 3-inch shells. Spread the top as smooth as possible. Transfer to the oven and bake until the mixture begins to bubble, about 5 to 10 minutes. Set aside to cool to room temperature. Using the tines of a fork, drizzle with the melted chocolate. The caramel will boil over; cool the tarts and then pop them in the oven for a few minutes. The shell will pop right out of the mold.

Bitter Chocolate Shortbread ✳

Adapted from a basic shortbread made by Maria Helm at Plumpjack Café in San Francisco, we use this shortbread for our Hazelnut Sandwich Cookies. Of course they're so good, you can just eat them without the hazelnut filling.

½ pound (2 sticks) unsalted butter, at room temperature
⅓ cup confectioners' sugar
1½ teaspoons vanilla extract
1 teaspoon salt
1⅓ cups all-purpose flour
⅔ cup unsweetened cocoa

Preheat the oven to 350 degrees. Line a baking sheet with parchment paper.

Place the butter and sugar in the bowl of a mixer fitted with a paddle and beat until creamy. Add the vanilla and mix to combine. Add the salt, flour, and cocoa and mix until well incorporated. Place the dough between sheets of parchment paper or wax paper and roll out until ¼ inch thick. Cut out 1½-inch circles. Transfer to prepared sheet and bake until the centers are dry when touched, about 10 to 12 minutes. Let cool on the sheets. Store in an airtight container up to 2 weeks.

MAKES 48 COOKIES

Hazelnut Filling

4 tablespoons unsalted butter, at room temperature
2 tablespoons praline paste (available at specialty food stores)
Pinch salt
1 cup confectioners' sugar
½ teaspoon vanilla extract
Milk

¼ cup ground toasted hazelnuts (see box on page 36; see box below)

◆ GRINDING NUTS COOL TOASTED NUTS TO ROOM TEMPERATURE, PLACE IN FOOD PROCESSOR, AND PULSE UNTIL DESIRED CONSISTENCY. ◆

Place the butter, praline paste, and salt in the bowl of a mixer fitted with a paddle and mix until light and fluffy. Add the confectioners' sugar and mix to combine. Add the vanilla. Add the milk, a few drops at a time, if necessary to make spreading consistency.

Place a dollop of the filling in the middle of the underside of a Bitter Chocolate Shortbread. Top with another shortbread. Some filling will show on the sides. Roll the sides in the ground hazelnuts. Repeat. Store in an airtight container up to 2 days.

MAKES ENOUGH TO FILL 24 COOKIES

TO FINISH AND ASSEMBLE:

1. Make a pool of Caramel Sauce slightly off center in a dessert plate.
2. Place a Caramelized Hazelnut Tart in the center of the plate.
3. Top with Chocolate Semi-Freddo.
4. Garnish with hazelnut sandwich cookies.

SERVES 12

Lime and Mango Tart with Zesty Lime Curd and Broiled Mangoes

*D*uring the winter months, when we miss the color, variety, and smell of fresh fruits, citrus and mangoes help us survive. Limes are at a peak and are a natural foil to the sweetness and sensuous texture of the mangoes.

Pasta Frolla

½ cup sugar
Chopped zest of 1 lemon
Chopped zest of 1 orange
2¾ cups all-purpose flour
½ teaspoon salt
⁷⁄₁₆ pound (1¾ sticks) unsalted butter, cool but not straight
*   from the fridge*
2 large eggs
1 tablespoon vanilla extract

Place the sugar and zests in the bowl of a mixer fitted with a paddle and mix for 3 to 5 minutes. Add the flour and salt and mix to combine. Add the butter and mix until just smaller than pea-size. Add the egg and vanilla and mix until it is a shaggy mass. Place the mass on a lightly floured work surface and gather together with your hands, rubbing the board with the mass to pick up the scraps. Pat into a neat and tidy mass, wrap in plastic wrap, and refrigerate for at least 1 hour and up to 3 days or freeze up to 2 months.

Preheat the oven to 375 degrees.

To form tart shells: Dust a work surface with flour. Gently form the dough into 12 flat disks; take care not to overwork the dough. Beginning in the middle of the circle, and using short but firm strokes, roll up toward 12 o'clock. Turn clockwise and repeat and continue turning and rolling until the dough

is about ½ inch larger than the tart shell. Place the dough in twelve 3-inch tart pans or molds, taking care to lay the dough into the "corners" of the pan, between the sides and the bottom. Gently press into the sides to define the edges. Using your thumb, clean off the edges by pushing the dough against the edge of the pan or mold to cut off excess.

Line the dough with aluminum foil and top with a heavy layer of rice, beans, or pie weights. Transfer to the oven and bake until the dough is set and dry to the touch, about 10 to 12 minutes. Remove the aluminum foil and bake until golden, about 3 to 4 minutes. Set aside to cool to room temperature.

Lime Curd ✳

1 cup sugar
2 large eggs
6 large egg yolks
½ cup fresh lime juice
½ cup fresh lemon juice
4 tablespoons unsalted butter (optional)
Chopped zest of 2 limes

Place the sugar, eggs, and egg yolks in a bowl and mix to combine. Add the juices and mix to combine. Place the bowl over a hot-water bath over medium heat. Leave a whisk in the bowl and stir every 5 minutes or so, stirring a total of 15 to 20 minutes or until the mixture is thick and begins to leave tracks. Off heat, add the butter, if using, and stir to melt. Pour through a strainer and discard the solids. Add zest and cool to room temperature. Cover and refrigerate at least 1 hour and up to 4 days.

MAKES ABOUT 2 CUPS

Lime and Mango Tart ✳

*P*inched from a Jim Dodge recipe, this custard balances mango creaminess with lime acidity.

1 cup heavy cream
4 large egg yolks
4 large eggs
¾ cup sugar
½ cup fresh lime juice
¼ cup fresh lemon juice
Chopped zest of 3 limes
3 large mangoes, pureed and strained
1 large mango, cut in ½-inch dice
Twelve 3-inch parbaked Pasta Frolla shells (page 183)

Preheat the oven to 325 degrees.

Place the cream in a small pan and bring to a boil over high heat. Place the egg yolks, eggs, sugar, and juices in a bowl and mix to combine. Add the cream and mix. Pour through a strainer and discard the solids. Add the lime zest and pureed mango. Fold in the diced mango.

Pour into prepared Pasta Frolla shells and bake until the edges are slightly souffléed and the middle is dry to the touch, about 15 to 18 minutes. Cover and refrigerate up to 2 days.

Broiled Mango

2 mangoes, thinly sliced
2 tablespoons sugar

Preheat the broiler.

Place the mangoes on a baking sheet, sprinkle with the sugar, and place under the broiler. Cook until the sugar bubbles and caramelizes, about 4 minutes. Set aside.

TO FINISH AND ASSEMBLE:

1. Place a Lime and Mango Tart in the center of a dessert plate.
2. Fan the Broiled Mangoes on top of the tart.
3. Garnish with Lime Curd.

SERVES 12

Butter-Basted Apple Tart
with Currants and Walnuts,
Cornmeal Dough, and Zaletti

Susan and Bob Jasse of Alyson's Orchard in Walpole, New Hampshire, have had great success working with heirloom apple varieties, among them the lyrically named Cox Orange Pippin and Maiden's Blush. We developed this tart to show off apples like these old-fashioned beauties, which hold their shape during cooking and are less juicy than more common varieties. If you aren't fortunate enough to get the Jasses' apples, you can use any hard eating apple, like Macoun. These beauties are what it's all about: crisp, snappy, juicy, sweet/tart, and never sour. They are a delight to eat, cook with, smell, and look at but they need to be cooked soon after they are picked: They don't store well. If you can't get Macouns, use Granny Smiths.

Zaletti (Italian Cornmeal Cookie) ✳

These odd little cookies are very crunchy and grainy the first day and then mellow as time goes by. The currants are traditionally soaked in rum and drained before being added, but you can eliminate this step.

⅔ cup sugar
Chopped zest of 2 lemons
2 cups stone-ground yellow cornmeal
1 cup all-purpose flour
½ teaspoon salt
1 teaspoon baking powder
⅜ pound (1½ sticks) butter, cold
⅔ cup currants
2 large eggs
1 large egg yolk
2 teaspoons vanilla extract
Confectioners' sugar, for dusting

Preheat the oven to 350 degrees. Line a baking sheet with parchment paper.

Place the sugar and lemon zest in the bowl of a mixer fitted with a paddle and mix for 3 to 5 minutes. Add the cornmeal, flour, salt, and baking powder and mix to combine. Add the butter, a little bit at a time, and mix until it almost forms a dough. Add the currants, eggs, egg yolk, and vanilla and mix until just combined.

Form into 4 logs. Flatten to the width of a necktie and slice down the middle. Slice at 1-inch intervals on a diagonal, creating the traditional diamond shape. Transfer to the oven on prepared sheet and bake until the bottoms are brown, about 20 minutes. Allow to cool on the sheet, toss in confectioners' sugar, and then store in an airtight container up to 2 weeks.

MAKES ABOUT 48 COOKIES

Cornmeal Blitz Dough

*T*his really should be made in a food processor. If you do it by hand, you heat up the dough too fast and it won't be as tender.

¾ cup stone-ground yellow cornmeal
1¼ cups all-purpose flour
1 teaspoon salt
½ pound (2 sticks) unsalted butter, chilled
¼ cup ice water
¼ cup orange juice, cold

Place the cornmeal, flour, and salt in a bowl and toss to combine. Add the butter, a little at a time, and mix until it resembles coarse gravel. Add the water and juice and mix just until the dough comes together in a shaggy mass.

Place the mixture on a floured surface and form into a rectangle. Fold into thirds, like a letter going into an envelope. Roll into a tube and flatten slightly with the seam on the bottom. Cut into 2 portions, flatten each portion into a square, cover with plastic wrap, and refrigerate at least 1 hour and up to 2 days.

Apple Hash ✳

*B*asically a chunky, sloppy applesauce. Granny Smith apples work well.

6 tart apples, peeled, cored, sliced into sixteenths
⅔ cup sugar
¼ cup light brown sugar
½ teaspoon salt
3 tablespoons unsalted butter
Chopped zest of 2 lemons
2 tablespoons currants
¼ cup chopped, toasted walnuts (see box on page 36)
Pinch ground cinnamon

Place the apples, sugars, salt, and butter in a medium-size saucepan over medium heat and cook until the apples are just tender, about 20 minutes. Add the zest, currants, walnuts, and cinnamon. Use immediately or cover and refrigerate up to 4 days.

MAKES ABOUT 6 CUPS

TO FINISH AND ASSEMBLE:
6 tart apples, peeled, cored, and sliced
2 tablespoons unsalted butter, melted

1. Preheat the oven to 400 degrees.
2. Portion the Cornmeal Blitz Dough into 6 pieces and roll each into a 7-inch circle (see Yeasted Dough, page 157).
3. Portion the Apple Hash in the center of the shell.
4. Top with the sliced apples and fan them over the Apple Hash, in shingles, overlapping and tucking as you go. Baste with the butter, transfer to the oven, and cook for 10 minutes, basting occasionally. Lower the oven temperature to 350 degrees and bake, basting every 10 minutes, until the apples are tender, about 20 minutes.
5. Cool, and serve with the Zaletti on the side.

SERVES 6

Layered Banana Cream Pie with Pecan Goo on Sweet Banana Cake with Toffeed Pecans and Tuiles

One long night, Olives server Floyd (who's real name is Mark, but there were too many Marks at Olives, so Olivia renamed him Floyd) came into the pastry kitchen with a plea from a guest: "I want *that* banana cream pie." Todd, a man of few words, offered lots of hand motions and a few key words: *layered, pecans, creamy, lots of banana,* and then he went back to cook on the line. This is what we worked out and we never got any complaints.

Banana Cake ✳

¼ pound (1 stick) unsalted butter, at room temperature
1 cup plus 2 tablespoons sugar
3 large eggs, separated
3 overripe bananas, mashed
½ cup buttermilk
4 ounces white chocolate, melted (optional)
2 cups all-purpose flour
1 teaspoon baking soda
1 teaspoon baking powder
1¼ teaspoons salt
½ cup chopped toasted pecans (see box on page 36)

Preheat the oven to 350 degrees. Line a 9 x 13-inch pan with parchment paper, or grease and flour 12 muffin cups.

Place the butter and 1 cup of the sugar in the bowl of a mixer fitted with a paddle and mix until light and fluffy. Add the egg yolks and beat well. Add the bananas and buttermilk and mix to combine: It'll look broken, but it's OK. Add the white chocolate, if using.

(continued)

Place the egg whites and the remaining 2 tablespoons sugar in a bowl and whip until stiff but not dry.

Place the flour, baking soda, baking powder, salt, and pecans in a bowl and toss to combine.

Add half the egg whites to the banana mixture, then half the flour mixture. Repeat. Spread into the prepared pan or muffin cups. Transfer to the oven and bake until golden and the cake springs back to the touch, about 35 minutes, or 22 to 26 minutes for the muffins. Cool to room temperature in the pan.

Toffee Cookie Crust

1 cup unsalted butter
1 cup light brown sugar
1 teaspoon salt
2 large egg yolks
2 cups all-purpose flour

Place the butter and sugar in a bowl and mix until creamed. Add the salt and egg yolk and mix until well incorporated. Add the flour and mix until just combined. Cover and refrigerate at least 30 minutes and up to 3 days.

Preheat the oven to 350 degrees.

Lightly flour a work surface. Divide the dough into 12 portions. Roll out the dough onto a lightly floured board and fit into twelve 3½-inch tart shells. Chill at least 20 minutes.

Line the dough with aluminum foil and top with a heavy layer of rice, beans, or pie weights. Transfer to the oven and bake until the dough is set and dry to the touch, about 10 to 12 minutes. Remove the aluminum foil and bake until golden, about 3 to 4 minutes. Set aside to cool to room temperature.

Pecan Goo

*G*oo is made with honey. It's never quite solid: When you pull it, you get threads. It's almost too sweet, so you can't eat much of it. You can use it in a chocolate tart or on ice cream.

4 tablespoons unsalted butter
2 tablespoons honey
1 tablespoon sugar
¼ cup light brown sugar
Pinch salt
1 heaping cup lightly toasted chopped pecans (see box on page 36)
1 tablespoon heavy cream
½ teaspoon vanilla extract

Place the butter, honey, sugars, and salt in a saucepan and bring to a boil over medium heat, stirring all the while. Allow to boil for 5 minutes undisturbed. Off heat, add the pecans and stir to coat. Add the cream and vanilla and stir to combine. Transfer to a plastic container and refrigerate up to 2 weeks.

MAKES ABOUT 2 CUPS

Pastry Cream

This makes a good filling for fruit tarts, cream puffs, and éclairs, and can be baked or left as is.

2¼ cups milk
1 vanilla bean, split and scraped
½ cup plus 1 tablespoon sugar
6 tablespoons cornstarch
1 large egg
4 large egg yolks
4 tablespoons unsalted butter
½ teaspoon salt

4 bananas, mashed with a potato masher

Place 2 cups of the milk and the vanilla bean in a pot and bring to a boil over high heat. Off heat, steep for 1 hour. Place the sugar and cornstarch in a small bowl and mix to combine. Add the egg, egg yolks, and the remaining ¼ cup milk and mix until it forms a smooth paste.

Remove the bean from the milk. Rinse and reserve for Vanilla Sugar (see box on page 47). Bring the milk back to a boil and pour over the yolk mixture, whisking all the while. Strain the mixture through a sieve back into the cooking pot, taking care to scrape the mixing bowl well. Bring back to a boil over medium heat, whisking all the while, and cook until the mixture thickens.

Transfer to the bowl of a mixer fitted with a paddle. Add the butter and salt and mix on low speed until it is room temperature, about 20 minutes. Place plastic wrap directly on the surface and refrigerate at least 1 hour and up to 2 days. Fold in the mashed bananas.

MAKES ABOUT 6 CUPS

Toffeed Pecans ✳

½ pound plus 2 tablespoons (2¼ sticks) unsalted butter
1¾ cups plus 2 tablespoons sugar
1 tablespoon salt
3½ cups pecan halves

Line a baking sheet with parchment paper.

Place the butter in a small saucepan over medium-low heat and cook until melted. Add the sugar and salt and stir briskly until the mixture comes together. Add the nuts and cook, stirring the nuts evenly and constantly, until the sugar caramelizes and coats the nuts.

When the sugar has turned a beautiful oak brown, carefully pour the hot mass onto the prepared sheet and quickly separate the nuts with forks or tongs. When the nuts have cooled completely, transfer to an airtight container and store for 3 to 5 days or freeze up to 2 weeks.

MAKES 5 CUPS

Tuile Twist ✳

5/16 pound (1¼ sticks) unsalted butter, melted
1 cup confectioners' sugar
½ cup plus 2 tablespoons sugar
½ teaspoon vanilla extract
½ teaspoon almond extract
¼ teaspoon salt
5 large egg whites
1 cup plus 2 tablespoons all-purpose flour

Preheat the oven to 350 degrees. Line a baking sheet with parchment paper.

Place the butter and sugars in the bowl of a mixer fitted with a paddle and mix until smooth, creamy, and warm, but not hot, about 3 to 4 minutes. Add the vanilla, almond extract, and salt and mix until incorporated.

Add half the egg whites and mix until completely incorporated. Scrape down the bowl, add half the flour, and mix until completely incorporated. Scrape down the bowl and repeat with the remaining egg whites and flour. Cover and refrigerate until spreadable but not liquidy, about 30 minutes.

Place 1 teaspoonful of the mixture on the prepared baking sheet and, using the back of a spoon, form into a strip 1 inch wide and 4 inches long. Place 2 inches apart. Repeat until the baking sheet is full. Return the remaining mixture to the refrigerator.

Transfer the baking sheet to the oven and bake until the cookies are dry to the touch, about 8 minutes. Remove from the oven and immediately, one by one, wrap around the handle of a wooden spoon like a tube. Set aside to cool. Repeat with the remaining batter. Cool and place in an airtight container for up to 1 week.

MAKES 24 TO 30 TUILES

Boozy Caramel Sauce ✳

2 cups sugar
½ cup water
½ teaspoon salt
1 cup heavy cream
1 tablespoon vanilla extract
1 tablespoon bourbon

Place the sugar, water, and salt in a small saucepan and bring to a boil over high heat. Cook without stirring until the mixture begins to color, about 4 to 5 minutes. When the mixture is tea-colored, stir lightly with a wooden spoon to even out the coloring. Continue cooking, stirring occasionally, until it turns a dark mahogany color, about 3 to 5 minutes.

Bubbles will rise and when they just start to break up, quickly and carefully drizzle in the cream. It will sputter and splatter and come to a boil at first, but just continue adding the cream slowly and steadily, stirring all the while. Off heat, add the vanilla and bourbon. Set aside to cool to room temperature. Cover and refrigerate at least 2 hours and up to 3 days.

Just before serving, gently reheat over low heat, stirring all the while.

MAKES ABOUT 1 PINT

Chantilly Cream ✳

*2 cups heavy cream
Up to 2 tablespoons sugar
½ teaspoon vanilla extract*

Place a large stainless steel bowl in the freezer for at least 20 minutes.

Place the cream, sugar, and vanilla in the bowl and whip with a large whisk until medium peaks form, about 3 to 5 minutes. You can also machine whip for 2 minutes and then whip the rest by hand. Use immediately or cover and refrigerate no more than 3 hours.

TO FINISH AND ASSEMBLE:

2 bananas, sliced on the bias

1. Preheat the oven to 350 degrees.
2. Divide Pecan Goo among the Toffee Cookie Crust shells. Transfer to the oven and bake until they bubble in the center, about 5 to 7 minutes. Let cool to room temperature. (This step can be done 24 hours in advance.)
3. Portion the Banana Cake among 12 plates.
4. Place the cooled Toffee Cookie Crust shells on top of the Banana Cake.
5. Divide the Pastry Cream among the shells.
6. Pipe Chantilly Cream on top so that it looks like a sundae.
7. Sprinkle Toffeed Pecans over the top.
8. Garnish with sliced bananas (above) and Tuiles and drizzle with Boozy Caramel Sauce.

SERVES 12

Mango Tarte Tatin with Pastry Cream and Chocolate Pastry

On one of Todd's many sojourns as a guest chef, he wanted to serve the Mango Tarte Tatin. When he wrote up the menu, however, he couldn't remember all the elements of the original recipe. He just made it up as he went along. His improvisation was so much better than the original, it became part of the Olives menu.

The cocoa in the Blitz dough has a fruity flavor that complements tropical flavors of the mango and coconut.

Chocolate Blitz

When the recipe for Chocolate Blitz was misplaced, pastry whizzes Maria Wharton and Heather Macdonald discovered that their memories were not very good. But we learned that a bad memory can be a good thing, because what they came up with was leaps and bounds beyond the original. We wanted delicate, we wanted durable, we wanted cocoa black, and above all else, we wanted great taste. And they delivered.

We had never heard of Blitz, a fast puff paste of sorts, until we read Nick Malgieri's recipe. It blisters like puff paste and tastes like puff paste, but you don't get height, which is just perfect for this recipe.

¾ teaspoon salt
4 cups plus 2 tablespoons all-purpose flour
⅓ cup unsweetened cocoa
3 tablespoons sugar
⅜ pound plus 1 tablespoon (1⅝ sticks) unsalted butter, chilled
⅓ cup ice water

Place the salt, flour, cocoa, and sugar in a bowl and toss to combine. Add the butter, a little at a time, and mix until peanut-sized. Just before it binds together, add the water and toss to combine.

(continued)

On a floured surface, push together to make a mass. Flatten into a 12 x 18-inch rectangle. Fold into thirds, like a letter going into an envelope.

Turn the rectangle so the shape is long end away from you. Roll up jellyroll-style and flatten slightly with the tail on the bottom. (The thinner this mixture is when refrigerated, the easier it will be to roll out when cold and firm.) Cut in half, cover with plastic wrap, and refrigerate. Freeze half. This recipe makes twice as much as you need, but the process is so time-consuming that we always make a larger batch and freeze it.

Roll out to ⅛ inch thick and cut out 12 circles to fit mouth of mold (see page 206): You are making a top that will later become the bottom. Cover and refrigerate for at least 1 hour or freeze until ready to use, up to 2 months.

Coconut Pastry Cream

> 1¼ cups milk
> 1 cup canned, unsweetened coconut milk
> 1 vanilla bean, split and scraped
> ½ cup plus 1 tablespoon sugar
> 6 tablespoons cornstarch
> 1 large egg
> 4 large egg yolks
> 2 tablespoons unsalted butter
> ½ teaspoon salt
> 1 cup sweetened shredded coconut
> 2 ounces melted semisweet chocolate

Place 1 cup of the milk, the coconut milk, and the vanilla bean in a pot and bring to a boil over high heat. Off heat, steep for 1 hour. Place the sugar and cornstarch in a small bowl and mix to combine. Add the egg, egg yolks, and the remaining ¼ cup milk and mix until it forms a smooth paste.

Remove the vanilla bean from the milk. Rinse and reserve for Vanilla Sugar (see box on page 47). Bring the milk back to a boil and pour over the yolk mixture, whisking all the while. Strain the mixture through a sieve back into the cooking pot, taking care to scrape the mixing bowl well. Bring back to a boil over medium heat, whisking all the while, and cook until the mixture thickens.

Transfer to the bowl of a mixer fitted with a paddle. Add the butter and salt and mix on low speed until it is room temperature, about 20 minutes. Place plastic wrap directly on the surface and refrigerate at least 1 hour and up to 2 days. Fold in the coconut.

Transfer a fourth of the Coconut Pastry Cream to a small bowl and fold in the chocolate.

MAKES ABOUT 4 CUPS

Boozy Caramel Sauce ✳

2 cups sugar
½ cup water
½ teaspoon salt
1 cup heavy cream
1 tablespoon vanilla extract
1 tablespoon bourbon

Place the sugar, water, and salt in a small saucepan and bring to a boil over high heat. Cook without stirring until the mixture begins to color, about 4 to 5 minutes. When the mixture is tea-colored, stir lightly with a wooden spoon to even out the coloring. Continue cooking, stirring occasionally, until it turns a dark mahogany color, about 3 to 5 minutes.

Bubbles will rise and when they just start to break up, quickly and carefully drizzle in the cream. It will sputter and splatter and come to a boil at first, but just continue adding the cream slowly and steadily, stirring all the while. Off heat, add the vanilla and bourbon. Set aside to cool to room temperature. Cover and refrigerate at least 2 hours and up to 3 days.

Just before serving, gently reheat over low heat, stirring all the while.

MAKES ABOUT 1 PINT

Caramelized Mangoes

The mangoes must be cooked in two batches so that they caramelize properly.

2 cups sugar
6 tablespoons water
12 medium mangoes, peeled and cut into 2 large front and back panels
*   and two small side panels; cut each large panel into thirds*
6 tablespoons unsalted butter

Cook half the sugar with 3 tablespoons of water until tea-colored. Do not stir. Swirl pan to even the cooking/coloring. When the sugar is evenly browned, add 6 mangoes. Allow to cook undisturbed for 3 minutes. Stir to mix sugar. Cook, stirring gently until most of the juices have evaporated, approximately 5 minutes. Add 3 tablespoons of the butter; stir to coat. Transfer to a large platter and cool. Repeat with remaining ingredients.

TO FINISH AND ASSEMBLE:

1. Preheat the oven to 375 to 400 degrees.
2. Arrange the Caramelized Mangoes in the bottom of a flat-bottomed ovenproof cereal-style bowl.
3. Top with 2 tablespoons of the Boozy Caramel Sauce. (Remember that the bottom will be the top: It gets cooked upside down and flipped over later.)
4. Pipe the chocolate coconut pastry cream around the edges of the mango.

5. Place 3 tablespoons of the Coconut Pastry Cream onto the Boozy Caramel Sauce. Spread gently to coat and don't fuss too much. (The recipe can be prepared 24 hours in advance up to this point.)

6. Place the frozen Chocolate Blitz dough onto the prepared tart. Transfer the tart to the oven and bake until the sides are bubbling, about 16 to 18 minutes. Set aside for 3 minutes.

7. Run the tip of a paring knife around the sides of the molds. Using a flat metal spatula to hold the crust securely in the tart, quickly invert onto a plate and remove the mold. Adjust the mangoes if necessary. Serve with additional Boozy Caramel Sauce.

SERVES 12

Cakes

Apple-Topped Gingerbread with Hot Apple-sauce and Cinnamon Ice Cream

The Apple-Topped Gingerbread is complete when it comes out of the oven, but we couldn't resist gilding the lily with applesauce and cinnamon ice cream.

Cinnamon Ice Cream ✳

1 cup heavy cream and 3 cups milk (or 2 cups milk and 2 cups
heavy cream; see page 57)
½ teaspoon salt
3 cinnamon sticks

⅔ cup sugar
8 large egg yolks
2 teaspoons vanilla extract

1 teaspoon ground cinnamon (optional)
2 teaspoons sugar (optional)

Place the cream, milk, salt, and cinnamon sticks in a saucepan and bring to a boil over high heat. Allow to steep for 1 hour.

Place the sugar, egg yolks, and vanilla in a large bowl and mix to combine. Return the cream to a boil and pour over the egg mixture, whisking all the while. Allow to sit 5 minutes. Pour through a strainer and discard the solids. Chill in an ice bath. When cool, cover and refrigerate. Transfer to an ice cream maker and freeze according to the manufacturer's instructions.

You can mix the cinnamon and sugar together and add it to the ice cream after it has cooled but before it is frozen. Don't add it earlier: The cinnamon acts as a starch and will give you glue if added during the cooking process.

MAKES 2 QUARTS

Apple-Topped Gingerbread ✳

This is also delicious served with sweetened whipped cream.

¼ pound (1 stick) unsalted butter, at room temperature
½ cup sugar
½ cup molasses
½ cup sour cream or full-fat yogurt
2 large eggs, at room temperature
1½ cups all-purpose flour
1 teaspoon baking powder
½ teaspoon baking soda
½ teaspoon salt
1½ teaspoons ground ginger
1 tablespoon finely grated fresh gingerroot
2 hard apples (such as Granny Smith, Baldwin, or Macoun), peeled, cored, and thinly sliced
2 tablespoons unsalted butter, melted

Preheat the oven to 350 degrees. Lightly grease and flour a 9-inch cake pan.

Place the butter and sugar in a bowl of a mixer fitted with a paddle and mix until creamy. Add the molasses and mix until creamy. Add the sour cream and mix until creamy.

Add the eggs, one at a time, beating well after each addition. Add the flour, baking powder, baking soda, salt, ground ginger, and gingerroot and mix just to combine.

Place the batter in the prepared pan and smooth down. Place the apples on top in a circle, shingle style, around the edges of the cake. Transfer the cake to the oven and bake until the center is set and springs back under pressure, about 30 minutes, basting every 10 minutes with the melted butter. Serve warm or at room temperature. Cover and store at room temperature up to 2 days.

Applesauce ✳

*J*f you peel the apples first no straining is necessary. Why would you leave the skins on if they'll only cause you heartache later? Because if you choose a red apple, your applesauce will come out a muted rose color, which is quite appealing (just a little fruit humor!).

2 pounds tart apples, cored, peeled, and quartered
2 tablespoons sugar
2 tablespoons light brown sugar
Pinch salt
½ cup apple cider
1 to 2 cinnamon sticks

Place all the ingredients in a large pot and cook, covered, over medium heat for 20 minutes. Stir and continue to cook for 20 to 30 minutes. Repeat one to two times or until the apples are falling-apart soft, about 40 to 60 minutes. Remove and discard the cinnamon sticks. Transfer the mixture to a food processor fitted with a steel blade and puree or strain the mixture through a sieve. Cover and refrigerate up to 1 week.

MAKES ABOUT 1 QUART

TO FINISH AND ASSEMBLE:

1. If necessary, heat the Applesauce.
2. Slice the Apple-Topped Gingerbread into 10 pieces.
3. Garnish with Cinnamon Ice Cream and hot Applesauce.

SERVES 10

Real Good, Real Basic Pound Cake with Seasonal Fruit Compote and Burnt Orange Ice Cream

*T*ruly good pound cake is an exercise in patience. It's just you, your paddle, and the ingredients. The much-maligned pound cake is often considered too plain, too simple, too dull. Not to us: It's just not complicated. In fact, we think it's elegant. It deserves the best seasonal fruits as an accompaniment. The Burnt Orange Ice Cream has incredible depth of flavor.

Burnt Orange Ice Cream ✳

*T*he idea for this came from *Walking on Walnuts*, an autobiographical book sprinkled with great recipes, by painter, poet, and pastry chef Nancy Ring.

4 cups orange juice
¾ cup Cointreau
1¼ cups sugar
⅓ cup water
1¼ cups heavy cream
3 cups milk
12 egg yolks
½ teaspoon salt
4 tablespoons finely chopped orange zest

Place the orange juice and Cointreau in a saucepan and bring to a boil over medium-high heat; cook until reduced by half, about 6 to 8 minutes. Set aside to cool.

Place ¾ cup of the sugar and the water in a small skillet and cook on high heat, stirring occasionally, until caramelized and mahogany-colored, about 5 minutes. Slowly add the cream, being careful for splattering. Add the milk and bring to a boil.

Place the remaining ½ cup sugar, egg yolks, and salt in a bowl and mix to combine.

Pour the milk mixture over the sugar-egg mixture, whisking all the while. Pour through a strainer into a container and discard the solids. Chill in an ice bath. Add the zest, transfer to an ice cream maker, and freeze according to manufacturer's instructions.

MAKES JUST LESS THAN 2 QUARTS

Pound Cake ✳

When you are mixing this, be sure to beat well: The mixture must be well aerated. Beat at least 3 minutes before adding the first egg and then beat for 3 minutes between each addition.

This is best served the day *after* it is cooked. For a delectable change in taste and texture, prick the top with a toothpick and douse with ½ cup of maple syrup or lemon syrup (⅓ cup lemon juice and ⅓ cup confectioners' sugar brought to a boil and cooled) right after it comes out of the oven.

1 pound (4 sticks) unsalted butter, at room temperature
1¾ cups sugar (or light brown sugar or a combination of both)
1 tablespoon vanilla extract
5 large eggs, at room temperature
2½ cups all-purpose flour
¾ teaspoon salt
¾ cups toasted ground walnuts (see box on page 36) or chocolate chips
   or dried fruits, including cherries, apricots, or raisins (optional)

Preheat the oven to 350 degrees. Grease and flour an 8- to 9-inch loaf pan.

Place the butter in a mixing bowl and mix until light and fluffy. Add the sugar and mix until well combined and smooth. Add the vanilla and the eggs, one

at a time, beating well and scraping down the bowl after each addition. Add the flour and salt and mix until just combined. Fold in the nuts, if using.

Pour the batter into the prepared pan and transfer to the oven. Bake until a toothpick inserted comes out clean, about 1 hour. Set aside for 10 minutes.

Turn the cake out on a wire rack and allow to cool completely before wrapping in aluminum foil, plastic wrap, or a resealable plastic bag. Store at room temperature for 4 to 5 days or freeze up to 2 weeks. If it becomes stale, it make great toast.

If flavoring the pound cake with syrup, douse liberally with the syrup when still warm, before unmolding.

Seasonal Fruit Compotes ✳

FALL/WINTER:

1 cup apple cider
1 cup orange juice
½ cup dried cherries
½ cup dried apricots
½ cup dried figs
2 tablespoons golden raisins
2 tablespoons currants
Zest of 2 oranges
Zest of 1 lemon
1 cinnamon stick
2 apples, peeled and cut into 1-inch dice
2 pears, peeled and cut into 1-inch dice
½ teaspoon salt
1 cup toasted, coarsely chopped walnuts (see box on page 36) (optional)

Place the cider and orange juice in a medium-size saucepan and cook until warmed, about 2 to 3 minutes. Off heat, add the dried fruits, zests, and cinnamon sticks and let sit until the fruit is plumped, about 30 minutes.

(continued)

Add the diced apples and pears and mix to combine. Place on medium heat and cook until tender, about 15 minutes. Add the salt.

Cool to room temperature and add the nuts, if using. Cover and refrigerate up to 1 week.

MAKES ABOUT 1 QUART

SPRING:

1 pound rhubarb, cut into 1-inch dice
Zest of 2 oranges
½ vanilla bean, split and scraped
½ cup sugar
2 pints strawberries, rinsed, hulled, and quartered
½ to 1 teaspoon fresh lemon juice

Place half the rhubarb, the orange zest, vanilla bean, and sugar in a medium-size pot and cook, stirring occasionally, over medium heat until the rhubarb begins to fall apart, about 8 minutes. Add the remaining rhubarb and cook until almost fork tender, about 4 to 5 minutes. Off heat, add the strawberries, stir well, and cool. Add lemon juice. Cover and refrigerate up to 1 week.

MAKES ABOUT 1 QUART

SUMMER:

6 large peaches, peeled, pitted, and cut into ½-inch slices
2 tablespoons sugar
½ teaspoon fresh lemon juice
1 pint fresh raspberries, rinsed

Place the peaches, sugar, and lemon juice in a pot and cook until just fork tender, about 2 to 3 minutes. Off heat, immediately add the raspberries. Cover and refrigerate up to 24 hours.

MAKES ABOUT 1 QUART

TO FINISH AND ASSEMBLE:

1. Slice the Pound Cake into 1-inch slabs. Cut each piece in half.
2. Arrange 2 to 3 pieces on a dessert plate.
3. Spoon the Seasonal Fruit Compote over the Pound Cake.
4. Garnish with a scoop of Burnt Orange Ice Cream.

SERVES 6 TO 8

Cranberry Upside-Down Cake with
Caramel Semi-Freddo and Pecan Shorts

This is the ultimate upside-down cake. The oft-heard complaint about these homey cakes is that they're too sweet. Here the tart cranberry flavor shines through the sugar and is beautiful to boot! We played with bits of orange and pecan in the cake for added dimensions of color and texture. The semi-freddo, with its burnt-sugar sweetness and creamy texture, is an unexpected complement to the cake, and the Pecan Shorts finish the plate with a nice, dry bite.

Caramel Semi-Freddo ✳

1¾ cups sugar
½ cup water
½ cup heavy cream

5 large eggs
10 large egg yolks
½ teaspoon salt
¼ cup prepared strong coffee

3½ cups heavy cream, whipped
1½ teaspoons vanilla extract

To make the caramel: Place the sugar and water in a saucepan and cook over medium heat until it turns a deep mahogany color, about 4 to 5 minutes. Do not stir: Gently swirl to even out the color. Slowly add the cream and stir very gently but be careful, it will splatter. Set aside but keep warm.

Place the eggs, egg yolks, salt, and coffee in a bowl over a hot-water bath and whisk until warmed. Add the caramel and whisk until the mixture is homogenous, thick, light in color, and has the consistency of soft whipped cream, about 4 to 5 minutes.

(continued)

Immediately pour the mixture into the bowl of a mixer fitted with a whisk and whip on high speed until it cools to room temperature, about 5 to 8 minutes.

Place the whipped cream in a large mixing bowl and fold in one quarter of the caramel-egg mixture. Add the vanilla and all the whipped cream to the caramel-egg mixture and gently fold to combine. Pour into a 6- to 8-cup freezer container and freeze at least 4 hours and up to 5 days.

MAKES ABOUT 2 QUARTS

Cranberry Upside-Down Cake   *

TOPPING:

4 tablespoons unsalted butter, at room temperature
¼ cup sugar
6 tablespoons light brown sugar
1 bag (12 ounces) fresh cranberries

CAKE:

4 tablespoons unsalted butter, at room temperature
½ cup brown sugar
Zest of one lemon, chopped
Zest of one orange, chopped
2 large eggs
½ cup milk
1 teaspoon vanilla extract
1¼ cups all-purpose flour
1½ teaspoons baking powder
½ teaspoon salt
½ bag (6 ounces) fresh cranberries
½ cup chopped, toasted pecans (see box on page 36)

Line a 9-inch cake pan with parchment paper. Grease and flour the sides and bottom.

To make the topping: Place the butter and sugars in a bowl and mix until creamy. Spread on the bottom of the prepared cake pan. Pour the cranberries over the butter mixture and press in.

To make the cake: Place the butter, sugar, and zests in the bowl of a mixer fitted with a paddle and mix until light and fluffy. Add the eggs, one at a time, scraping down the bowl after each addition. Add the milk and vanilla. It'll look slightly broken, but just go on. Add the flour, baking powder, and salt and mix until almost combined. By hand, fold in the cranberries and pecans. (Be sure to do this by hand: If you mix them in a mixer they'll break down.) Spread gently over the cranberries in the cake pan. Transfer to the oven and bake until the cake's center springs back with a gentle push and the sides are bubbling and gooey, about 45 to 55 minutes. Allow to rest 15 minutes. Run a paring knife around the edge of the pan and place a platter or dinner plate face down over the cake.

Using a dish towel or pot holder to hold the bottom of the hot cake pan, invert the cake onto the plate. Remove the pan straight up. If it sticks a little bit, no sweat: Just move a few berries over the spot. Cut into 8 pieces.

Pecan Shorts ✳

¼ pound (1 stick) unsalted butter, at room temperature
⅓ cup confectioners' sugar, plus additional for tossing
½ teaspoon salt
1 teaspoon vanilla extract
1 cup all-purpose flour
⅓ cup finely ground toasted pecans (see box on page 36)

Preheat the oven to 350 degrees.

Place the butter and sugar in a bowl and mix until creamy. Add the salt and vanilla and mix to combine. Add the flour and pecans and mix until just combined.

(continued)

Form the dough into 1-inch balls (a no. 100 scoop is helpful) and place on an
ungreased baking sheet. Transfer the sheet to the oven and bake until the
bottoms are golden, about 10 to 12 minutes. Cool on the sheet. When they
have cooled completely, toss with confectioners' sugar. Store at room
temperature up to 2 days.

MAKES 2 TO 3 DOZEN

TO FINISH AND ASSEMBLE:

1. Place a piece of Cranberry Upside-Down Cake on a dessert plate.
2. Top with a scoop of Caramel Semi-Freddo.
3. Garnish with Pecan Shorts.

SERVES 8

Hot and Sassy Gingerbread with Ginger Crinkles, Cider Sauce, and Ginger Ice Cream

This is *not* a dessert for the meek or the mild. The snappy, spicy cake is paired and contrasted with candy-sweet, rich, gooey stuffed dates.

Ginger Ice Cream ✳

The ginger ice cream acts as a buffer to the fiery gingerbread: The casein in the milk is a natural fire extinguisher.

3 cups milk
1 cup heavy cream
¼ cup sliced fresh gingerroot, unpeeled
8 large egg yolks
⅔ cup Vanilla Sugar (see box on page 47)
¼ teaspoon salt
1 teaspoon vanilla extract

Place the milk, cream, and gingerroot in a small pot and bring to a boil over medium-high heat. Off heat, allow to steep for 1 hour.

Place the egg yolks, Vanilla Sugar, and salt in a mixing bowl and stir to combine. Bring the milk mixture back to a boil and carefully pour the boiling mixture over the yolk mixture, stirring all the while. Off heat, let sit for 5 minutes. Add the vanilla. Pour through a fine mesh strainer, discard the solids, and chill in an ice bath. Transfer to an ice cream maker and freeze according to manufacturer's instructions.

MAKES 5 CUPS

Glazed Stuffed Dates with Goop ✳

Although we include these on this dessert, we don't even list them on the menu description at Olives because date detractors wouldn't order the Hot and Sassy Gingerbread as a result. Our staff, on the other hand, loves these incredibly sweet, jammy, funky-looking, fun-to-make dates. Betcha can't eat two.

Muscovado sugar is grown in volcanic soil on an island off the tip of Africa.

STUFFED DATES:

STUFFED DATES:

⅓ cup ground, roasted walnuts (can substitute almonds, pecans, hazelnuts) (see boxes on pages 36 and 181)
1 teaspoon light brown sugar
1 tablespoon egg white
Pinch salt
Splash vanilla extract
12 to 15 Medjool dates, split lengthwise and pitted

GOOP:

2 tablespoons unsalted butter, at room temperature
6 tablespoons muscovado (available at specialty markets) or dark brown sugar
1 large egg yolk
2 tablespoons plain yogurt
¼ teaspoon vanilla extract
½ cup all-purpose flour
Pinch salt
¼ teaspoon baking soda
Pinch baking powder

GLAZE:

⅓ *cup confectioners' sugar*
3 to 5 drops water

To stuff the dates: Place the nuts, sugar, egg white, salt, and vanilla in a bowl and mix well. Place a small amount of the mixture into the opening in the dates and close up; it's OK if they don't reclose completely, they're supposed to be "stuffed"!

Preheat the oven to 350 degrees.

To make the goop: Place the butter and sugar in a bowl and mix until creamy. Add the egg yolk and yogurt and mix until well combined. Add the vanilla. Place the flour, salt, baking soda, and baking powder in a small bowl and mix to combine. Add the flour mixture and mix just to combine. With wet hands, spread the goop on the stuffed dates. It's OK if it's spotty and thin in some areas and thicker in others. Transfer to the oven and bake until they color and dry, about 12 minutes. Cool to room temperature.

To make the glaze: Place the confectioners' sugar in a bowl and slowly add water until it makes a smooth paste. Loosen with a few more drops of water if necessary. Drizzle wildly over the cooled baked dates.

Cover and store at room temperature up to 2 days.

Ginger Crinkles ✳

*T*hese cookies are soft and chewy with a distinct sugar crunch the first day. The second day they are mellow and soft with a sweet exterior. Left unwrapped they become great dippers. The recipe actually comes from a magazine article from about twenty years ago entitled something like "Greatest Cookie Jar Classics." The formula has been changed a bit and the original lost but not forgotten.

⅜ pound (1½ sticks) unsalted butter, at room temperature
1 cup plus 2 tablespoons brown sugar
1 egg
⅓ cup molasses
Zest of 1 lemon, chopped
2 tablespoons fresh ginger, grated
2 cups all-purpose flour
½ cup whole wheat flour
2 teaspoons baking soda
¾ teaspoon salt
1½ tablespoons ground ginger
1 teaspoon ground cinnamon
Extra-coarse sugar for rolling

Preheat the oven to 350 degrees. Line a baking sheet with parchment paper.

Place butter and brown sugar in the bowl of a mixer fitted with a paddle and beat until creamy. Add the egg and beat well. Scrape down the sides of the bowl and add the molasses, lemon zest, and fresh ginger. Blend. Add the flours, baking soda, salt, ground ginger, and cinnamon. Mix just to combine. Scoop the dough into small balls (using a no. 100 scoop) and toss to coat in coarse sugar. Space 2 inches apart on the prepared baking sheet. Bake at 350 degrees until the sides are set and the centers still soft, about 8 to 10 minutes. Bake only one pan at a time in the middle of the oven to ensure the distinctive "crinkle" tops. Cool on the baking sheet and store in an airtight container.

MAKES 24 TO 30 COOKIES

Hot and Sassy Gingerbread   *

One guest complained that this was too hot, but be forewarned: If you want just plain old gingerbread, make the Apple-Topped Gingerbread (page 211) without the apples. Served warm, Hot and Sassy Gingerbread has got buzz, bite, and heat.

You can top the raw batter with poached fruits, sliced apples or pears, or applesauce, just chill the batter first to enable the fruits to stay suspended. Bake as directed. Serve warm with butter or sweetened whipped cream or chilled with homemade Applesauce (page 213).

½ teaspoon salt
1½ teaspoons ground cinnamon
2 tablespoons ground ginger
¼ teaspoon ground cloves
½ teaspoon powdered mustard
½ teaspoon black pepper
½ teaspoon white pepper
¼ cup chopped crystallized ginger
¼ pound (1 stick) unsalted butter
¾ cup light brown sugar
2 large eggs, at room temperature
⅔ cup molasses
2½ cups all-purpose flour
2 teaspoons baking soda
1 cup boiling water

Preheat the oven to 350 degrees. Grease a 9-inch cake pan.

Place the salt, cinnamon, ginger, cloves, mustard, black pepper, white pepper, and crystallized ginger in a mixing bowl fitted with a paddle and mix for 2 minutes. Add the butter and mix until well creamed. Add the brown sugar and mix well. Scrape down the bowl and add the eggs, one at a time, mixing well after each addition. Add the molasses. The mixture may appear broken but just keep going, it will come together.

Place the flour and baking soda in a small bowl and mix to combine. Add half the flour mixture and then ½ cup of the boiling water and combine well. Repeat and mix until well combined. The batter will be quite loose.

Pour into the prepared pan and transfer to the oven. Bake until the top is dry, shiny, and springs back to the touch, about 25 to 35 minutes. Cover and store at room temperature up to 2 days.

Cider Sauce

4 cups apple cider
1 cinnamon stick
½ cup sugar
5 teaspoons cornstarch
¼ teaspoon salt
⅓ cup fresh lemon juice
½ teaspoon vanilla extract

Place the cider and cinnamon stick in a pot and bring to a boil over high heat. Cook until reduced by half, about 20 minutes. Strain and discard the cinnamon stick. Return to a boil.

While the cider is boiling, place the sugar, cornstarch, salt, and lemon juice in a bowl and mix to combine. Gradually pour the sugar mixture into the cider, stirring all the while. Bring back to a boil, add the vanilla, and set aside to cool. Cover and refrigerate up to 2 days.

MAKES 2½ CUPS

TO FINISH AND ASSEMBLE:

1. If necessary, heat the Hot and Sassy Gingerbread.
2. Cut gingerbread into 8 portions.
3. Puddle Cider Sauce in the center of the plate.
4. Place gingerbread on top of Cider Sauce.
5. Garnish with Ginger Ice Cream.
6. Serve with Glazed Stuffed Dates with Goop.
7. Serve with Ginger Crinkles.

SERVES 8

Many-Layered Lemon Cake

*L*emon rules at Olives. Our lemon devotees mean business and so do we.

Lemon Curd *

> *4 large eggs*
> *15 large egg yolks*
> *2¼ cups sugar*
> *1½ cups strained fresh lemon juice*
> *¼ pound (1 stick) unsalted butter*

Place the eggs, egg yolks, sugar, and lemon juice in a double boiler over low heat and cook until thickened, about 15 minutes. Stir occasionally with a wire whisk to promote even cooking. Raise the heat to medium high and cook, stirring constantly, until the mixture becomes thickened and tracks.

Off heat, add the butter and stir to combine. Pour through a strainer and discard the solids. Cool to room temperature, cover, and refrigerate at least 1 hour and up to 3 days.

MAKES ABOUT 4 CUPS

Lemon Custard

his has a lighter lemon flavor than we usually use, but it works well with all the other lemon elements.

1½ cups heavy cream
4 large eggs
2 large egg yolks
3 tablespoons cornstarch
¾ cup sugar
¾ cup fresh lemon juice

Preheat the oven to 300 degrees. Lightly grease two 9-inch flan rings.

Place the cream in a small saucepan and bring to a boil over high heat. Place the remaining ingredients in a bowl and pour the hot cream over them, stirring all the while. Pour through a strainer and portion into the flan rings. (It is very important to use a flat baking pan so the rings won't "leak." If you don't have a flat pan, wrap the bottom of each ring in plastic wrap and then again in aluminum foil. You could also use two 9-inch cake pans.) Discard the solids. Transfer to the oven and bake until edges rise slightly and the center jiggles, about 18 to 20 minutes. Set aside to cool to room temperature. Cover and refrigerate at least 2 hours and up to 2 days.

Lemon Cake ✳

his moist butter cake is laced with lemon zest and enriched with coconut milk. The cake is doused with coconut milk syrup or lemon syrup and layered with lemon custard, lemon curd, and lemon buttercream. Coconut is pressed into the sides for textural interest and to bring out the coconut in the cake. The tart lemon flavor dominates but works well with the richness of the coconut.

Chopped zest of 4 lemons
¾ cup confectioners' sugar
1⅓ cups sugar
½ pound (2 sticks) unsalted butter, at room temperature
5 large eggs, separated
¼ teaspoon cream of tartar
1 teaspoon vanilla extract
3 cups all-purpose flour
1 tablespoon baking powder
1 teaspoon salt
1¼ cups unsweetened coconut milk

Preheat the oven to 350 degrees. Line three 9-inch cake pans with parchment paper.

To make the cake: Place the lemon zest, confectioners' sugar, and 1 cup of the sugar in the bowl of a mixer fitted with a paddle and mix for 3 to 5 minutes. Add the butter and beat until light and fluffy. Add the egg yolks and vanilla and beat well.

Place the flour, baking powder, and salt in a bowl and mix to combine. Add the flour mixture to the lemon mixture, alternately with the coconut milk, and mix until just combined.

Place the egg whites and cream of tartar in a bowl and whip with a mixer until the eggs just begin to foam. Gradually add the remaining ⅓ cup sugar and slowly increase the speed until it is high; whip until the mixture is stiff and shiny. Fold into the batter and spread into the prepared pans. Transfer to the oven and bake until golden at the edges and the center springs back easily, about 20 to 22 minutes. Set aside to cool in the pans. Remove the cake from the pan when cool.

Soaking Syrups

COCONUT MILK SYRUP:

1 cup canned unsweetened coconut milk
⅓ cup sugar
½ teaspoon vanilla extract

OR

LEMON SYRUP:

1 cup confectioners' sugar
1 cup fresh lemon juice

Combine all ingredients and mix well until the sugar is completely dissolved.

MAKES ABOUT 1 CUP

Lemon Buttercream

6 egg yolks
½ cup fresh lemon juice
½ teaspoon salt
½ cup plus 2 tablespoons sugar
⅞ pound (3½ sticks) unsalted butter
½ teaspoon vanilla extract

Place the egg yolks, lemon juice, salt, and sugar in a double boiler over medium heat and cook, whisking, until hot, light yellow in color, and thickened, about 6 minutes. Transfer to the bowl of a mixer fitted with a whisk attachment and whip on high speed until cool, about 4 to 5 minutes. Add the butter, 2 tablespoons at a time, and whip until smooth. Add the vanilla.

(continued)

237

If the mixture is too soft to spread, cover and refrigerate for 20 minutes. Scrape down the bowl and whip for 1 minute.

MAKES ABOUT 3 CUPS

TO FINISH AND ASSEMBLE:

2 cups toasted coconut (see box)

◆ TOASTING COCONUT: PREHEAT THE OVEN TO 325 DE-
GREES. SPREAD THE COCONUT IN AN EVEN LAYER ON A
BAKING SHEET, THEN TOAST IT ON THE TOP RACK OF THE
OVEN FOR 10 TO 15 MINUTES, STIRRING EVERY 5 MINUTES
TO ENSURE EVEN COLORING. LET COOL COMPLETELY BE-
FORE USING. ◆

1. Trim the tops of the Lemon Cake layers.
2. Bottom-side down, lay the first layer on a cake plate. Brush with either Soaking Syrup.
3. Lay on a Lemon Custard layer.
4. Spread with Lemon Curd.
5. Repeat steps 2 through 4.
6. Place third Lemon Cake layer, flat side up.
7. Douse with Soaking Syrup.
8. Cover the top surface with Lemon Buttercream, then frost the sides.
9. Press the toasted coconut into the sides. Refrigerate until the Lemon Buttercream is set, about 30 minutes and up to 1 day.

SERVES 12 TO 14

Espresso Torte

*T*his is a popular birthday cake at Olives and one of our favorites. The cake is moist and sweet: The Espresso Buttercream is bold enough to stand up to the most assertive chocolates, the Espresso Syrup adds another layer of flavor, and the Bitter Chocolate Shortbread adds a nice texture change and whimsy to the outside of the cake.

Old-Fashioned Sour Cream Chocolate Cake ✳

7 ounces bittersweet chocolate
⅜ pound (1½ sticks) unsalted butter
¾ cup sour cream or full-fat plain yogurt
1½ teaspoons baking soda
2½ cups sugar
1 tablespoon vanilla extract
½ teaspoon salt
3 large eggs
3 cups all-purpose flour
1½ cups hot water or prepared coffee

Preheat the oven to 350 degrees. Grease and flour two 9-inch cake pans.

Place the chocolate and butter in a double boiler and cook over medium heat until melted. Set aside.

Place the sour cream and baking soda in a small bowl, mix to combine, and set aside.

Place the sugar, vanilla, salt, and chocolate-butter mixture in the bowl of a mixer fitted with a paddle and mix until just combined. Scrape down the bowl. Add the sour cream mixture and mix until just combined. Scrape down the bowl.

Add the eggs, one at a time, and mix until just combined. Scrape down the bowl. Add 1 cup of the flour, ½ cup of the hot water or prepared coffee; 1 cup flour, ½ cup water; and the remaining 1 cup flour and ½ cup water, scraping down the bowl and stirring well after each addition. Do not overmix. Pour into the prepared pans and transfer to the oven. Bake until a toothpick inserted in the center comes out clean and the cake center springs back when pressed gently, about 25 to 30 minutes. Serve immediately or wrap and store at room temperature up to 3 days or freeze up to 2 weeks.

Espresso Syrup

1 cup brewed espresso
1 cup sugar

Place the coffee and sugar in a small pan and bring to a boil over high heat. Set aside to cool, cover, and refrigerate at least 20 minutes and up to 1 week.

MAKES 1⅓ CUPS

Espresso Buttercream

*B*asic buttercream with espresso flavoring.
To make this a chocolate buttercream, omit the coffee and add 6 ounces cooled, melted semisweet or bittersweet chocolate after the vanilla is added.

1 cup sugar
⅓ cup prepared coffee
Pinch salt
4 large egg whites
¼ teaspoon cream of tartar
1 pound (4 sticks) unsalted butter, at room temperature
*1 tablespoon coffee paste (dissolve 2 tablespoons espresso powder in 1
    tablespoon hot coffee)*
2 teaspoons vanilla extract

Place ¾ cup of the sugar, the coffee, and salt in a small pot and cook until it has reached the soft ball stage, about 236 to 240 degrees. Unless you are very experienced, use a candy thermometer.

While the coffee mixture is cooking, place the egg whites and cream of tartar in a bowl and whip with a mixer until the eggs just begin to foam. Gradually add the remaining ¼ cup sugar and slowly increase the speed until it is high; whip until the mixture is stiff and shiny.

Gently pour the sugar syrup down the inside of the bowl with the egg whites, all the while whipping on high speed. Continue whipping until the bottom of the bowl is cool to the touch, about 7 minutes.

While the mixer is still running, add the butter, in tablespoons, and mix until it is completely incorporated. Scrape down the bowl and add the coffee paste and vanilla. Use immediately or freeze up to 2 months.

MAKES 4½ CUPS

Bitter Chocolate Shortbread   ✳

½ pound (2 sticks) unsalted butter, at room temperature
⅓ cup confectioners' sugar
1½ teaspoons vanilla extract
1 teaspoon salt
1⅓ cups all-purpose flour
⅔ cup unsweetened cocoa

Preheat the oven to 350 degrees. Line a baking sheet with parchment paper.

Place the butter and sugar in the bowl of a mixer fitted with a paddle and beat until creamy. Add the vanilla and mix to combine. Add the salt, flour, and cocoa and mix until well incorporated. Place the dough between sheets of parchment paper and roll out until ¼ inch thick. But out 1½-inch circles or shapes, such as hearts, spades, diamonds, and clubs. Transfer to the oven on prepared sheet and bake until the centers are dry when touched, about 10 to 12 minutes. Let cool on the sheet. Store in an airtight container up to 2 weeks.

MAKES 36 TO 48 COOKIES

Semisweet Chocolate Ganache

8 ounces semisweet chocolate
1 cup heavy cream

Method One (to be used when you want to spread immediately): Place the chocolate in the top of a double boiler and cook until melted. Add the cream and stir until smooth.

Method Two (to be used if you want to pour immediately): Place the cream in a pan and bring to a boil over high heat. Place the chocolate in a bowl and pour the hot cream over it. Cover for 2 minutes. Whisk until smooth.

Both can be covered and refrigerated up to 1 week.

MAKES ABOUT 1¾ CUPS

TO FINISH AND ASSEMBLE:

1. Trim the top of the Old-Fashioned Sour Cream Chocolate Cakes.
2. Slice each layer in half horizontally.
3. Lay one layer, bottom-side down, on a cake plate.
4. Brush with Espresso Syrup.
5. Spread on Semisweet Chocolate Ganache.
6. Spread on Espresso Buttercream.
7. Repeat steps 3 to 6.
8. Repeat steps 3 to 6.

9. Turn the fourth cake layer bottom-side up and place on Espresso Buttercream.
10. Brush with Espresso Syrup.
11. Spread Espresso Buttercream on top and sides of cake.
12. Randomly drizzle Semisweet Chocolate Ganache on top of cake, allowing it to drip down the sides.
13. Stick the Bitter Chocolate Shortbreads randomly over the cake.
14. Refrigerate until the buttercream sets, about ½ hour.

SERVES 12 TO 14

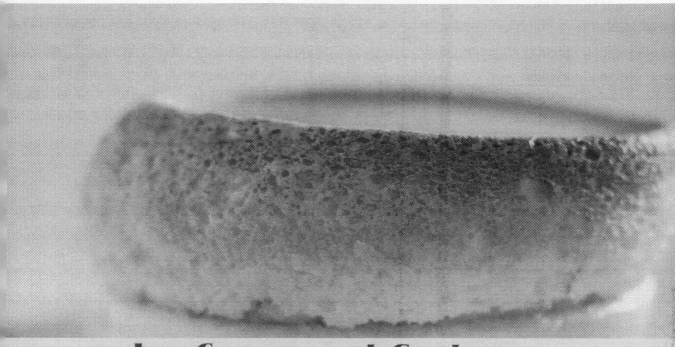

Ice Cream and Sorbets

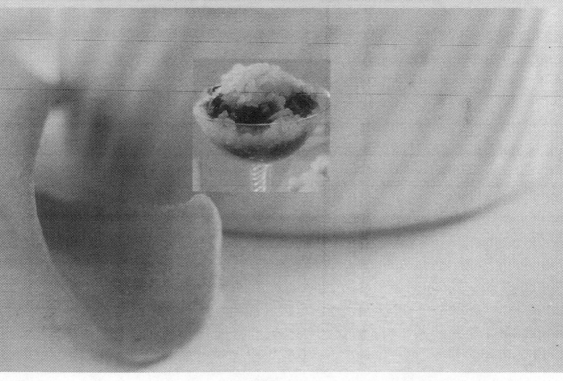

Turtle Sundae:
Caramel and Vanilla Bean Ice Creams in a Pecan Short Shell with Chocolate and Caramel Sauces, Salted Pecan Bark, Caramel Turtles, Chantilly Cream, and Salted Pecans

When we purchased an ice cream machine, we envisioned a fun summertime dessert that would catch people's eyes as it traveled across the dining room at Olives. This sundae is literally built from the ground up—and one of the few at Olives that is so structured and so architectural. The temptation is to dismantle this dessert with your fingers. Just dig in; all the elements are finger-friendly.

The Pecan Short Shell is the foundation, or the dish, of the sundae. We paint the bottom of the shell with milk chocolate and fill it with Vanilla Bean and Caramel Ice Creams, Chantilly Cream, Chocolate and Caramel Sauces, Caramel Turtles, Salted Pecans, and Salted Pecan Bark! We tried to scale this down because it was so large, but it just didn't work, so share!

Caramel Ice Cream ✳

The high percentage of sugar makes the amount of salt essential. You might look at it and think it's too much salt but it cuts the sweetness of the sugar. Don't even think about reducing it.

¾ cup sugar
Rounded ½ teaspoon salt
⅓ cup water
¾ cup heavy cream
2¼ cups milk
¼ vanilla bean, split
2 teaspoons vanilla extract
4 egg yolks

Place ½ cup of the sugar, salt, and water in a medium-size pan over medium heat and cook, stirring occasionally, until it reaches a deep mahogany brown, about 5 minutes. Slowly and carefully add the cream, taking care as it will splatter as it boils. Add the milk and vanilla bean and return to a boil. Off heat, allow to steep for 1 hour.

Remove the vanilla bean, taking care to rub all of the seeds into the pot. Rinse the pod and dry for future use.

Place the vanilla, egg yolks, and the remaining ¼ cup sugar in a small bowl and mix to combine. Return the cream mixture to a boil and slowly add it to the egg mixture, whisking all the while. Off heat, let stand for 5 minutes. Pour through a fine-mesh strainer and cool in an ice bath. Discard the solids.

Transfer to an ice cream machine and freeze according to manufacturer's instructions.

MAKES ABOUT 1 QUART

Vanilla Bean Ice Cream ✳

3 cups milk
1 cup heavy cream
1 vanilla bean, split
8 large egg yolks
⅔ cup Vanilla Sugar (see box on page 47)
¼ teaspoon salt
1 teaspoon vanilla extract

Place the milk, cream, and vanilla bean in a small pot and bring to a boil over medium-high heat. Off heat, allow to steep for 1 hour.

Remove vanilla bean, taking care to rub all of the seeds into the pot. Rinse the pod and dry for future use.

Place the egg yolks, Vanilla Sugar, and salt in a mixing bowl and stir to combine. Bring the milk mixture back to a boil and carefully pour the boiling mixture over the egg yolk mixture, stirring all the while. Off heat, let sit for 5 minutes. Add the vanilla. Pour through a fine-mesh strainer and chill in an ice bath. Discard the solids. Transfer to an ice cream maker and freeze according to manufacturer's instructions.

MAKES ABOUT 2 QUARTS

Pecan Short Shells ✳

½ pound (2 sticks) unsalted butter, at room temperature
⅔ cup confectioners' sugar
1 teaspoon salt
2 teaspoons vanilla extract
2 cups all-purpose flour
⅔ cup finely ground toasted pecans (see boxes on pages 36 and 181)

Preheat the oven to 350 degrees.

Place the butter and sugar in a bowl and mix until creamy. Add the salt and vanilla and mix to combine. Add the flour and pecans and mix until just combined.

Lightly flour work surface. Divide the dough into 12 sections. Roll out the dough onto a lightly floured board and fit into twelve 3½-inch tart shells. Chill at least 20 minutes.

Line the dough with aluminum foil and top with a heavy layer of rice, beans, or pie weights. Transfer to the oven and bake until the dough is set and dry to the touch, about 10 to 12 minutes. Remove the aluminum foil and bake until golden, about 3 to 4 minutes. Set aside to cool to room temperature.

MAKES 12

Chocolate Sauce ✳

¼ pound (1 stick) unsalted butter
4 ounces semisweet chocolate
2½ tablespoons prepared coffee
2½ tablespoons corn syrup
½ cup sugar
½ cup unsweetened cocoa powder
Pinch salt
½ cup plus 2 tablespoons heavy cream
½ teaspoon vanilla extract

Place the butter and chocolate in the top of a double boiler and cook until both have melted. Add the coffee and corn syrup and stir to combine.

Add the sugar, cocoa powder, and salt and stir to combine. Add the cream and stir until all sugar grains have dissolved. Off heat, add the vanilla. Set aside to cool, cover, and refrigerate up to 2 weeks.

MAKES ABOUT 2 CUPS

Boozy Caramel Sauce ✳

2 cups sugar
½ cup water
½ teaspoon salt
1 cup heavy cream
1 tablespoon vanilla extract
1 tablespoon bourbon

Place the sugar, water, and salt in a small saucepan and bring to a boil over high heat. Cook without stirring until the mixture begins to color, about 4 to 5 minutes. When the mixture is tea-colored, stir lightly with a wooden spoon to even out the coloring. Continue cooking, stirring occasionally, until it turns a dark mahogany color, about 3 to 5 minutes.

Bubbles will rise and when they just start to break up, quickly and carefully drizzle in the cream. It will sputter and splatter and come to a boil at first, but just continue adding the cream slowly and steadily, stirring all the while. Off heat, add the vanilla and bourbon. Set aside to cool to room temperature. Cover and refrigerate at least 2 hours and up to 3 days.

Just before serving, gently reheat over low heat, stirring all the while.

MAKES ABOUT 1 PINT

Salted Pecan Bark ✳

*I*f you cannot find salted pecans, simply toss the pecans in ¼ teaspoon salt and ¼ cup hot water (to dissolve the salt) and spread on a baking sheet. Preheat the oven to 350 degrees and bake until dry, about 8 to 10 minutes. Cool to room temperature before proceeding.

1 pound El Rey milk chocolate, melted
1½ cups salted pecans, toasted (see box on page 36)

Line a baking sheet with parchment paper.

Place the chocolate and pecans in a bowl and stir until the pecans are well coated. Transfer to the prepared sheet and spread as thinly as the pecans allow. Refrigerate until firm. Break into playing card–sized pieces (not perfect rectangles, mind you, but generous shards), cover, and refrigerate until firm, at least 30 minutes and up to 2 days.

Caramel Turtles ✳

*T*he basic elements of the turtle are caramel, pecans, and salt. Salt? Yep. The salt cuts the sweetness of the caramel and pumps up the impact of the chocolate.

The truth is, we make our own caramels and we do not use Kraft caramels. We thought this would make the project more accessible to home cooks.

24 Kraft caramels
120 jumbo pecan halves (about 5 cups) plus additional for garnish,
    toasted (5 for each turtle, 2 turtles per dessert) (see box on page 36)
8 ounces milk chocolate, melted

Preheat the oven to 350 degrees. Line a baking sheet with parchment paper.

Position 5 pecans on the baking sheet, underside down, nub end in, with the tips almost touching, in a loose star shape.

Place the caramels on a baking sheet in the oven and bake until they are pliable, about 2 minutes. Roll each caramel into a ball and place it in the center of the nuts, just covering the nub ends of the pecans. Place in the oven and bake until the caramel just melts, about 2 minutes. Cool on the sheet.

Run a flat metal spatula under the turtles to loosen them from the parchment. Using a small paper pastry bag or the tip of a teaspoon, drizzle the chocolate in a star shape in between the turtle's legs, neck, and over its back, making sure to cover the caramel. Refrigerate.

MAKES 24 TURTLES

Chantilly Cream ✳

2 cups heavy cream
Up to 2 tablespoons sugar
½ teaspoon vanilla extract

Place a large stainless steel bowl in the freezer for at least 20 minutes.

Place the cream, sugar, and vanilla in the bowl and whip with a large whisk until medium peaks form, about 3 to 5 minutes. You can also machine whip for 2 minutes and then whip the rest by hand. Use immediately or cover and refrigerate no more than 3 hours.

TO FINISH AND ASSEMBLE:

1. Drizzle the Boozy Caramel Sauce and Chocolate Sauce randomly over dessert plates.
2. Place a Pecan Short Shell in the middle of each plate.
3. Place 2 scoops of Caramel Ice Cream in the shell and 1 scoop Vanilla Bean Ice Cream.
4. Pipe the Chantilly Cream on top of the ice cream so that it looks like a sundae.
5. Randomly drizzle the Boozy Caramel Sauce and Chocolate Sauce on top of the Chantilly Cream.
6. Sprinkle the plate with salted pecans, if desired.
7. Position the Caramel Turtles in the Chantilly Cream so they look like they are climbing.
8. Garnish with Salted Pecan Bark.

SERVES 12

Cranberry-Lime Sorbet with Walnut Rugelach

*T*his refreshing sorbet is adapted from a dessert made by Rita Garubba at Leathercoat, a now-defunct restaurant in The Plains, Virginia. It comes out differently in each ice cream machine: some add a lot of air, while others freeze slower but firmer. The color may be deep red or various shades of pink.

Cranberry-Lime Sorbet ✳

1 cup sugar
2½ cups water
2½ cups fresh cranberries (1 bag)
¾ cup fresh lime juice
Grated zest of 1 lime

Place the sugar and 1 cup of the water in a small saucepan and bring to a boil over high heat. When the sugar has dissolved, add the cranberries and return to a boil. Cook until the cranberries pop, about 4 minutes. Set aside to cool. Place in a blender and puree until smooth.

Add the remaining 1½ cups water, lime juice, and lime zest and puree. Refrigerate until cold.

Transfer to an ice cream maker and freeze according to the manufacturer's instructions.

If you are not using an ice cream maker, place the mixture in a shallow bowl, cover, and place in the freezer and stir every hour. When the mixture is frozen and you are just about to serve it, cut it into 10 to 12 pieces and place them in the bowl of a food processor fitted with a steel blade. Pulse until the frozen chunks break up and the mixture has a creamy but solid consistency.

Serve immediately.

MAKES 1½ QUARTS

Walnut Rugelach ✳

*T*he rugelach adds texture and richness to the plate. The walnut also has a tannic bite that plays on the astringent edge of the cranberry. If you're not making these to serve with sorbet, they're equally delicious filled with cinnamon sugar or your favorite jam.

½ pound (2 sticks) unsalted butter, at room temperature
8 ounces cream cheese, at room temperature
1 teaspoon salt
2 cups all-purpose flour
1 cup sugar

FILLING:
½ cup chopped roasted walnuts
or
⅓ cup cinnamon sugar
or
⅓ cup jam

Preheat the oven to 325 degrees. Line a baking sheet with parchment paper.

Place the butter in a bowl and mix until creamed. Add the cream cheese and mix until creamed. Add the salt and flour and mix until just combined.

Cover with plastic wrap and refrigerate at least 1 hour and up to 2 days. Cut the dough into 4 equal portions.

Generously sprinkle a work surface with sugar. One portion at a time, roll the dough out into a 10-inch disk. If necessary, add more sugar to prevent the dough from sticking to the work surface.

Cut each disk into 8 wedges and place 1 tablespoon of the filling over the dough. Roll each wedge up croissant style, starting at the widest edge and making sure the tail is tucked under the body of the cookie.

(continued)

Place the cookies 2 inches apart on the prepared baking sheet and transfer to the oven. Bake until the bottoms are medium brown, about 12 to 15 minutes. Cool on the sheet. Store in an airtight container at room temperature up to 2 days.

MAKES 32 RUGELACH

TO FINISH AND ASSEMBLE:

1. Portion the Cranberry-Lime Sorbet into serving dishes.
2. Garnish with Walnut Rugelach.

SERVES 8

Lime Granita with Raspberry Crush and Citrus Shortbreads

When Paige was growing up, her mom used to take her and her two sisters shopping and when the girls had had enough, she'd leave them at the soda fountain in the department store. All three ordered raspberry lime rickeys, and considered themselves to be very adult, very cool, very hip! She developed this updated version for those who want to re-capture that same feeling.

At the restaurant, we layer the granita in a tall glass with Raspberry Crush and serve it with a long spoon and two straws. If you don't have tall glasses, this will taste just as good in a bowl.

Lime Granita ✳

So zippy it should hurt.

2 cups water
1 cup sugar
2 cups fresh lime juice
2 tablespoons fresh lemon juice

Place a 9 x 13-inch shallow pan in the freezer at least 20 minutes before making this dessert.

Place the water and sugar in a small saucepan and bring to a boil over high heat. Set aside to cool to room temperature. Add the juices and stir well. Transfer to the frozen pan and return to the freezer for 30 minutes. Stir with a fork, being careful to get the edges. Continue freezing and stirring every 30 minutes until the mixture starts to look slushy and have little shards of ice, but not be frozen solid, about 1 to 1½ hours. Cover and freeze for up to 3 days. Stir again with the fork if necessary.

MAKES ABOUT 6 CUPS

Citrus Shortbread ✳

⅓ cup confectioners' sugar
Chopped zest of 1 lemon
Chopped zest of 1 orange
¼ pound (1 stick) unsalted butter, at room temperature
1 teaspoon vanilla extract
½ teaspoon salt
1 cup plus 2 tablespoons all-purpose flour

Preheat the oven to 350 degrees. Line a baking sheet with parchment paper.

Place the sugar and zests in the bowl of a mixer fitted with a paddle and mix for 3 to 5 minutes. Add the butter and mix until creamed. Scrape down the bowl, add vanilla, and mix just to combine. Add the salt and flour and mix just to combine.

To roll out into cookies: Form the dough into a disk and on a floured board roll out to ⅛-inch thickness. Dust off the excess flour and cut into shapes, such as hearts or circles, using a flour-dusted cookie cutter. Using a wide spatula, transfer the shapes to the prepared sheet and bake until the edges just begin to color, about 10 to 15 minutes. Set aside to cool on the sheet.

MAKES ABOUT 24 TO 36 COOKIES

Raspberry Crush ✳

2 pints fresh raspberries, rinsed
¼ to ⅓ cup sugar
1 teaspoon fresh lemon juice

Using your hand, gently crush ½ cup of the raspberries. Place the crushed and whole berries, sugar, and lemon juice in a bowl, mix to combine, and refrigerate at least 1 hour and up to 2 days.

MAKES ABOUT 3 CUPS

TO FINISH AND ASSEMBLE:

1. Portion three layers each of Lime Granita and Raspberry Crush into glasses.
2. Garnish with Citrus Shortbread.

SERVES 6 TO 8

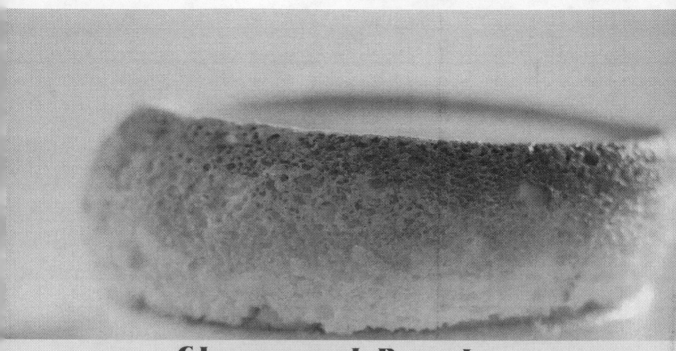

Cheese and Breads

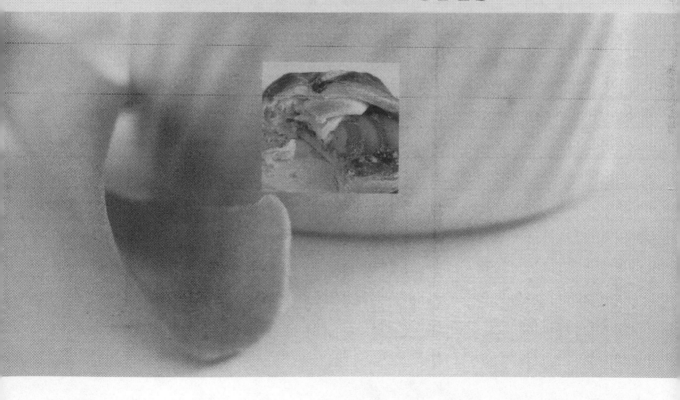

Blue Cheese Danish
with Port-Poached Pears

odd is a big fan of playing sweet against savory flavors. Like many of our best desserts, this one started as an experiment. We were working with a classic Danish dough and substituted blue cheese for the butter. Although we couldn't substitute one for one, we found that the blue cheese infiltrated the dough nicely. This item is great for brunch or dessert, a fun substitution for a cheese course.

Blue Cheese Danish Dough

he Danish dough demands some time, but may be made ahead and frozen.

⁵/₁₆ pound (1¼ sticks) unsalted butter
2 tablespoons all-purpose flour
6 tablespoons frozen blue cheese, the harder the better, crumbled

DOUGH:

2½ cups all-purpose flour
⅔ cup cake flour (not self-rising)
1 package (¼ ounce) active dry yeast
3 tablespoons sugar
Chopped zest of 1 lemon
1 teaspoon salt
1 large egg
1 large egg yolk
¾ cup cold milk
4 tablespoons unsalted butter, at room temperature

2 cups crumbled blue cheese, for assembly
1 egg yolk, for assembly

Place the butter and flour in the bowl of a mixer fitted with a paddle and mix until smooth but still cool, about 3 minutes. Mix in crumbled blue cheese; set aside.

To make the dough: Place all the ingredients in the bowl of a mixer fitted with a dough hook and mix until it forms a smooth dough. Knead for 4 to 5 minutes. Transfer to a floured board and roll into a 12 x 18-inch rectangle. Spread blue cheese mixture over two-thirds of the dough, fold uncovered third over the middle buttered third, and then the third buttered third back over the first (like folding a letter). Roll out again to a 12 x 18-inch rectangle, fold first third over second, and third back over first. Take care to brush all excess flour off the dough when folding (you don't want to interrupt the layers). Dimple the dough in one corner with one fingertip to mark your place in the process, cover, and refrigerate at least 30 minutes and up to 1 hour. Repeat the three-fold, dimple with 2 fingers, and set aside for 30 minutes. Repeat three-fold and dimple with 3 fingers. Done! Cover and refrigerate. Use within 1 day or freeze up to 6 weeks.

While the dough is chilling, make the Port-Poached Pears.

Lightly flour a board. Roll out the dough to a 12 x 18-inch rectangle. Cut into twelve 3 x 4-inch squares.

Remove the pears from the poaching liquid and drain. Slice each pear in half and slice lengthwise into 4 to 6 slices, taking care not to cut through the stem, and gently spread the slices into a fan shape. Place the fanned pear in the top right-hand corner and sprinkle liberally with blue cheese. Fold top left-hand corner into center. Fold bottom right corner into center and press gently so the dough adheres. Bring up bottom left corner into the center and press gently. The pear should be peeking out the top. Brush all the outside surfaces (not the pear) with egg yolk. Cover with a large empty plastic container or a 9 x 13-inch baking sheet and let sit 45 minutes to 1 hour and 15 minutes in a warm place (not hot!). You should see the layers starting to appear.

Preheat the oven to 350 degrees. Line a baking sheet with parchment paper.

Place the Danish on the prepared sheet, transfer to the oven, and bake until browned on the bottom, about 18 to 22 minutes.

Serve immediately.

Port-Poached Pears

*Y*ou can store the pears in the liquid for up to two days after it cools completely. The longer they sit in the liquid, the more wine-flavored they get and the deeper the blush.

3 cups red wine, such as Port, Merlot, or Zinfandel
½ cup sugar
2 black peppercorns
Zest of 1 lemon
6 ripe pears, peeled, cored

Place the wine, sugar, peppercorns, and lemon zest in a saucepan. Bring to a boil over medium-high heat and boil until the sugar has dissolved. Lower the heat to a simmer and gently slide the pears in, being careful to leave space between them. Rotate the pears once or twice during cooking and gently simmer until a knife tip slides easily in and out (like testing a boiled potato), about 10 to 15 minutes.

Remove and discard the peppercorns and lemon zest. Remove the pears from the poaching liquid and set aside to cool.

Return the liquid to a gentle boil over medium heat and cook until reduced to one-third. Transfer to a storage jar and refrigerate at least 1 hour and up to 3 days.

MAKES 6 PEARS AND 1½ CUPS LIQUID

Blue Cheese Shortbread　✳

*T*hese fragile crackerlike cookies are good served with earthy soups like potato or squash purée. You can add ¼ teaspoon cayenne for a kick.

7 tablespoons unsalted butter, at room temperature
7 tablespoons soft blue cheese, such as Gorgonzola or Roquefort
5 teaspoons sugar
1¼ cups all-purpose flour
¼ teaspoon salt
Pinch coarsely ground black pepper

Preheat the oven to 350 degrees. Line a baking sheet with parchment paper.

Place the butter and cheese in the bowl of a mixer fitted with a paddle and mix until creamy. Add the sugar, flour, salt, and pepper and mix until just combined. Form into a flat square, cover with plastic wrap, and refrigerate for 30 minutes. Roll on a lightly floured board to ¼ inch thick and cut into finger-sized rectangles. Prick with a fork and place on the prepared baking sheet.

Transfer to the oven and bake until just set but not colored, about 10 to 12 minutes. Cool on the sheet and use within 4 hours.

MAKES 36 COOKIES

TO FINISH AND ASSEMBLE:

1. Drizzle the reduced liquid from the Port-Poached Pears over the dessert plate.
2. Place the warm Blue Cheese Danish in the middle of the plate.
3. Garnish with the Blue Cheese Shortbread.

SERVES 12

Caramelized Walnut Tart
with Prunes, Onions, and Blue Cheese

As hard-core blue cheese lovers, we often experiment with blue cheeses; among our favorites are Maytag, Danablue, Roquefort, Gorgonzola, and our local fave, Great Hill Blue Cheese. Excluding the cheese, this tart is made of sweet elements and yet it pairs best with a salad. Served warmed for brunch or as a first course, it's fabulous. People are suspicious of the prune component, but it adds an intense sweetness that enhances the onion and makes a nice counterpoint to the salty cheese.

Flaky Dough

This is basically pie dough, and the only recipe in this book where you'll find shortening. Shortening does, we'll admit, have a place in life, albeit a small one: It melts at a higher temperature and blisters to give you a better flake. Flaky dough can be used instead of almost any sweet dough.

1½ cups all-purpose flour
½ teaspoon salt
1 teaspoon sugar
7 tablespoons unsalted butter
3 tablespoons cold shortening
2 to 3 tablespoons orange juice

Preheat the oven to 400 degrees.

Place the flour, salt, and sugar in a bowl and mix to combine. Add the butter and shortening and mix until the dough is in pea-sized pieces. Add the orange juice and toss until it resembles a shaggy dough. Press together to form a disk. Cover in plastic wrap and refrigerate at least 30 minutes and up to 2 days or freeze up to 2 weeks.

(continued)

Roll the dough out on a floured board to a circle about 12 inches, larger than a 10-inch tart shell.

Gently fit the dough into the mold, taking care to lift and press the dough into the "corners" of the tart shell. Trim the edges and press the flutes in to define the pattern. Refrigerate at least 30 minutes and, covered, up to 2 days.

Freeze at least 30 minutes and up to 2 days covered to minimize shrinkage. Line the dough with aluminum foil and top with a heavy layer of rice, beans, or pie weights. Place on a baking sheet, transfer to the oven, and bake for 15 minutes. Remove the aluminum foil and weights and bake until dry to the touch, about 4 to 5 minutes. Set aside to cool.

Prune Purée ✳

This also makes a great toast spread; its thickness makes it great on bagels, too.

8 ounces (2 cups) pitted prunes, roughly chopped
1½ cups orange juice
Zest of 1 lemon
Zest of 1 orange

Place all the ingredients in a medium-size pot and cook over medium heat for 20 minutes, stirring occasionally to prevent scorching. Continue cooking until most of the liquid has been absorbed, about 20 minutes. Transfer to a food processor and process until smooth. Cover and refrigerate up to 1 week.

MAKES ABOUT 1½ CUPS

Sautéed Onions

*N*ot exactly a common entry in a dessert book, Sautéed Onions can be added to savory dishes like burgers, omelettes and pizza. They are best prepared in a pan that isn't overcrowded.

3 tablespoons unsalted butter
2 large Vidalia or Spanish onions, peeled, sliced thinly
1 teaspoon salt
½ teaspoon pepper

Place the butter in a sauté pan over medium-high heat and when it has melted, add the onions and cook until soft and translucent, tossing every few minutes to ensure that they don't scorch on the bottom of the pan. Add salt and pepper. Cover and refrigerate up to 2 days.

Cool to room temperature.

MAKES ABOUT 2 CUPS

Caramelized Walnut Filling

*T*he smooth and edgy caramel pairs beautifully with the dry walnut.

½ cup sugar
3 tablespoons water
½ teaspoon salt
¼ teaspoon ground black pepper
6 tablespoons heavy cream
2 cups walnut halves, gently toasted (see box on page 36)

Place the sugar, water, salt, and pepper in a small saucepan and cook over medium-high heat, stirring occasionally, until it turns a light caramel color, about 5 to 7 minutes. Slowly add the cream, taking care not to splatter. Bring back to a boil, fold in the nuts, and use immediately.

MAKES 2½ CUPS

TO FINISH AND ASSEMBLE:

¾ cup blue cheese (or fontinella or sharp Cheddar), crumbled

1. Preheat the oven to 350 degrees.
2. Spread the Prune Purée on the bottom of the Flaky Dough shell.
3. Top with Sautéed Onions and spread to the edges.
4. Top with Caramelized Walnut Filling.
5. Crumble blue cheese on top of tart, just before baking.
6. Transfer to the oven and bake until it bubbles, about 10 to 12 minutes. Set aside to cool to room temperature. Cut into 8 portions.

SERVES 8

Gorgonzola Biscuits
with Poached Pear Reduction

Joe Brenner, the head chef at Olives, asked the pastry kitchen for some Gorgonzola Biscuits to accompany a beef dish. We liked the outcome so much, we couldn't wait for the special to run its course so we could use the biscuits for dessert. The savory Gorgonzola shortcake is not a traditional sweet, but it is quite satisfying at the end of a meal; although marbled with rich, oozy cheese, it is somehow, at the same time, delicate.

Serve this with a crisp apple, a pear, or a bunch of grapes and a glass of Port, Beaumes de Venise, or Muscat.

Poaching Liquid

The rich, sweet Port reduction works well in balancing the salt of the Gorgonzola biscuit. You can also drizzle this over ice cream, dip fruit into it, or use it to poach quince or apples.

3 cups red wine, such as Port, Merlot, or Zinfandel
½ cup sugar
2 black peppercorns
Zest of 1 lemon
6 ripe pears, peeled, cored, stem left intact

Place the wine, sugar, peppercorns, and lemon zest in a saucepan. Bring to a boil over medium-high heat and boil until the sugar has dissolved. Lower the heat to a simmer and gently slide the pears in, being careful to leave space between them. Rotate the pears once or twice during cooking and gently simmer until a knife tip slides easily in and out (like testing a boiled potato), about 10 to 15 minutes.

(continued)

273

Remove and discard the peppercorns and lemon zest. Remove the pears from the poaching liquid and set aside to eat another day, or use in Blue Cheese Danish with Port-Poached Pears (page 264).

Return the liquid to a gentle boil over medium heat and cook until reduced to one-third. Transfer to a storage jar and refrigerate at least 1 hour and up to 3 days.

MAKES ABOUT 1½ CUPS

Gorgonzola Biscuits

*O*nly a heathen would butter these beauties but, hey, there's nothing wrong with that. Buttered or not, eat these as soon as they come out of the oven. They do not store or reheat well, as the moisture in the cheese makes them rubbery.
These can also be served as an accompaniment to a beef dish or something equally intense.

*3 cups all-purpose flour
1½ tablespoons baking powder
¾ teaspoon salt
4 tablespoons unsalted butter, cold
3 ounces Gorgonzola cheese (about ⅔ cup), frozen, crumbled
1½ cups buttermilk or plain nonfat yogurt
3 ounces Gorgonzola cheese, at room temperature*

Preheat the oven to 425 degrees. Line a baking sheet with parchment paper.

Place the flour, baking powder, and salt in the bowl of a food processor fitted with a steel blade and pulse to combine. Add the butter and frozen Gorgonzola and pulse until they form pieces the size of a dried pea.

By hand, add the buttermilk and combine until the mixture is raggedy and just comes together.

(continued)

Lightly flour a work surface. Scrape the mixture onto the surface and dot it with the Gorgonzola cheese. Knead, but not more than 10 times. Do not overwork the dough. Flour your hands and pat the dough down to ½-inch thickness.

Using a floured 3- to 4-inch biscuit or cookie cutter, cut out 12 biscuits. Place the biscuits on the prepared baking sheet, transfer to the oven, and cook until the bottoms are the color of tea, about 12 to 18 minutes.

Serve immediately.

MAKES 12 BISCUITS

TO FINISH AND ASSEMBLE:

1. Drizzle the poached pear reduction over the Gorgonzola Biscuits.

SERVES 12

MAIL-ORDER SOURCES

◆ Dean and DeLuca
560 Broadway
New York, NY 10012
800-221-7714; www.deandeluca.com
Spices, cookware

◆ Penzey's Spices
P.O. Box 1448
Waukesha, WI 53187
414-574-0277; www.penzeys.com
Spices, vanilla extract

◆ Bridge Kitchenware
214 East Fifty-Second St.
New York, NY 10022
212-688-4220; www.bridgekitchenware.com
Cookware

◆ JN Kidds (Jack Shannon)
617-773-7388
Valrhona, El Rey chocolate, vanilla beans and extract

◆ Sur La Table
1765 Sixth Avenue South
Seattle, WA 98134-1608
1-800-243-0852; www.surlatable.com

◆ Williams-Sonoma
800-541-2233; www.williams-sonoma.com
Cookware, spices

INDEX

Page numbers in *italics* refer to illustrations.

METRIC EQUIVALENCIES

Liquid and Dry Measure Equivalencies

CUSTOMARY	METRIC
¼ teaspoon	1.25 milliliters
½ teaspoon	2.5 milliliters
1 teaspoon	5 milliliters
1 tablespoon	15 milliliters
1 fluid ounce	30 milliliters
¼ cup	60 milliliters
⅓ cup	80 milliliters
½ cup	120 milliliters
1 cup	240 milliliters
1 pint *(2 cups)*	480 milliliters
1 quart *(4 cups, 32 ounces)*	960 milliliters *(.96 liter)*
1 gallon *(4 quarts)*	3.84 liters
1 ounce *(by weight)*	28 grams
¼ pound *(4 ounces)*	114 grams
1 pound *(16 ounces)*	454 grams
2.2 pounds	1 kilogram *(1,000 grams)*

Oven Temperature Equivalencies

DESCRIPTION	°FAHRENHEIT	°CELSIUS
Cool	200	90
Very slow	250	120
Slow	300–325	150–160
Moderately slow	325–350	160–180
Moderate	350–375	180–190
Moderately hot	375–400	190–200
Hot	400–450	200–230
Very hot	450–500	230–260

Printed in the United States
By Bookmasters